Will They Like It or Use It?
The Development and Use of an Instrument to Measure Adult Learners' Perceived Levels of Computer Competence, Attitudes Toward Computers, and Attitudes Toward e-Learning Within a Corporate Environment

by

Steven R. Yacovelli

ISBN: 1-58112-288-8

DISSERTATION.COM

Boca Raton, Florida
USA • 2005

Will They Like It or Use It?
The Development and Use of an Instrument to Measure Adult Learners' Perceived Levels of Computer Competence, Attitudes Toward Computers, and Attitudes Toward e-Learning Within a Corporate Environment

Dissertation.com
Boca Raton, Florida
USA • 2005

ISBN: 1-58112-288-8

Will They Like It or Use It?
The Development and Use of an Instrument to Measure Adult Learners' Perceived Levels
of Computer Competence, Attitudes Toward Computers, and Attitudes Toward
e-Learning Within a Corporate Environment

by
Steven R. Yacovelli

An Applied Dissertation Submitted to the
Fischler School of Education and Human Services
in Partial Fulfillment of the Requirements
for the Degree of Doctor of Education

Nova Southeastern University
2005

Approval Page

This applied dissertation was submitted by Steven R. Yacovelli under the direction of the persons listed below. It was submitted to the Fischler School of Education and Human Services and approved in partial fulfillment of the requirements for the degree of Doctor of Education at Nova Southeastern University.

_____   _____
Gary Anglin, EdD   Date
Committee Chair

_____   _____
Todd Curless, PhD   Date
Committee Member

_____   _____
Maryellen Maher, PhD   Date
Executive Dean for Research and Planning

Acknowledgments

This research and subsequent results are dedicated to all my friends and family who supported me throughout this challenging process but most specifically to Richard Egan (the "Regan" in the Regan Computer Competence, Attitude, and Behavior Survey) for his undying love, support, and encouragement while I was "writin'."

I also wish to acknowledge the many individuals who helped to contribute to the results and success of this endeavor. Special thanks to my subject-matter experts for their helping "fine-tuning" the Regan Computer Competence, Attitude, and Behavior Survey. To the friends and colleagues who helped me "pry" into their businesses and disseminate the Regan Computer Competence, Attitude, and Behavior Survey, thank you for participating and being part of my "*N*." Thanks to Dr. Todd Curless for his support and advice on behalf of Nova Southeastern University. Finally, sincere gratitude to Dr. Gary Anglin, whose feedback and input have helped to greatly shape not only this work but me as an academic. Thank you.

Abstract

The Development and Use of an Instrument to Measure Adult Learners' Perceived Levels of Computer Competence, Attitudes Toward Computers, and Attitudes Toward e-Learning Within a Corporate Environment. Yacovelli, Steven R., 2005: Applied Dissertation, Nova Southeastern University, Fischler School of Education and Human Services. Databases/Educational Technology/Web Based Instruction/Technology Integration/Employee Attitudes/Self Efficacy

While "e-learning" has proliferated in our society, the problem exists that many corporations are delving into e-learning without fully understanding end users' self-reported computer competence or attitudes toward e-learning or computers in general, which could ultimately impact the success of e-learning at an organization. Studies have been done to examine these phenomena, but the vast majority center around the academic environment, and many are deemed archaic due to advances in technology. To examine this problem, this research study's goal was to develop a valid and reliable instrument that measures self-reported computer competence, overall attitudes toward computers, and attitudes toward e-learning appropriate for the corporate, adult learner.

The author reviewed various investigations that examined the definition of *attitudes toward computers* and the phenomenon of computer literacy. Little research exists that examines attitudes toward e-learning, and there is a lack of research for exploring all three phenomena on a nonacademic population.

The result of the study yielded the Regan Computer Competence, Attitude, and Behavior Survey. This instrument consists of five sections, totaling 130 items. Each section was comprised of entirely new questions or a combination of existing instruments whose validity and reliability have been explored in previous studies. The author employed a sample of 144 American adults working in a corporate or government organization. The author's analysis revealed that the Regan Computer Competence, Attitude, and Behavior Survey was a valid and reliable instrument. In addition, hypotheses were examined in this research study that looked at the correlation between certain variables and the three phenomena in question.

Table of Contents

Appendixes

Tables

Chapter 1: Introduction

Corporate America is undergoing a type of renaissance with regard to training and development. With the recent embracement of alternative technologies to accomplish training and development objectives, many companies are turning to media such as CD-ROM, the Internet, and private intranet in order to facilitate corporate training and education. The term being used throughout the business world and beyond is *e-learning*, and it is helping to revolutionize the way in which businesses educate their employees (Urban & Weggen, 2000).

In its infancy, the expectation for e-learning was rather high. According to the Commission on Technology and Adult Learning (2000), industry experts initially expected e-learning (specifically, Web-based training) to "surge by more than 900 percent between 1999 and 2003" (p. 10), but these high expectations did not materialize due to a variety of factors. Although the September 11, 2001, terrorist attacks on the United States and the economic recession afterwards continue to have an impact on businesses' expenditures on corporate training, corporate spending on employee training remains and e-learning still continues to transform most companies training landscape but not at the level in which it was initially expected (Thompson, Koon, Woodwell, & Beauvais, 2002). According to the American Society for Training and Development (ASTD), organizations were reportedly sending fewer employees to classroom courses and opting for e-learning instead for reasons of both cost savings measures and security (Thompson et al.). In a recent survey of 270 United States training organizations, almost 77% of these companies said they had increased their use of e-learning since September 11, 2001 (Thompson et al.). In addition, the latest data available from ASTD show that training delivered via learning technologies (e-learning) increased in a sample ($N = 476$)

of global training and development organizations analyzed in late 2002, between 15 and 29% and is projected to increase more in subsequent years (Sugrue, 2004). This utilization of learning technologies is not isolated to the United States: In 2002, Japanese organizations reported to be delivering 20% of training via technology, while Latin American organizations delivered approximately 3% of their training efforts via e-learning methods (Sugrue). Brennan (2003), a market research analyst whose area of expertise is corporate learning and performance, noted that "E-learning has entered the period of mass adoption. Training professionals realize that Web-based technologies will play a growing role in the way that training programs are created, managed, and delivered for the foreseeable future" (p. 6).

With the momentum of e-learning reshaping the corporate training world, its effective use and efforts to apply appropriate performance analysis prior to its implementation are documented few and far between. Identifying corporate organizations that are willing to share their e-learning strategies are rare (mostly due to the competitive nature of the private sector), but then finding those who are willing to share their experiences and that have applied performance analysis (such as conducting a thorough needs analysis of their learners) to their e-learning strategies is even more of a challenge. This, in turn, makes it difficult for an e-learning practitioner who wishes to apply sound, theoretical research toward his or her e-learning initiatives and instructional design based upon the experiences and successes of others.

Statement of the Problem

There are few if any studies done as to whether e-learning is right for a particular business environment from a learners' perspective. Many corporate educators are being charged to change their corporate training organizations to show financial benefits by incorporating alternative delivery technologies and not necessarily show the educational

advantages to the utilization of these new media or their appropriateness to the learners

within their respective corporate cultures (Rossett, 2002). Learners may not be ready or

have the skills to use these new delivery technologies, but corporate leaders want them to

use these delivery methods for the fiscal advantages they can bring to the company.

Urban and Weggen (2000) identified this advantage for organizations, noting that

> corporations save between 50-70 percent when replacing instructor-led training
>
> with electronic content delivery. Opting for e-training also means that courses can
>
> be pared into shorter sessions and spread out over several days so that the
>
> business would not lose an employee for entire days at a time. Workers can also
>
> improve productivity and use their own time more efficiently, as they no longer
>
> need to travel or fight rush-hour traffic to get to a class. (p. 10)

It is important to note that learners' perceptions about the characteristics of

instructional delivery media and their ability to learn using these media have been shown

to be key determinants in predicting student motivation and success in traditional

classrooms (Bandura, 1977; Clark & Sugrue, 2001; Coggins, 1988). Many researchers

noted that there is a definite correlation between successful implementation of new

technologies and the attitudes and opinions of the end users of that technology–in this

case the students (Davis, Bagozzi, & Warshaw, 1989; Zoltan & Chapanis, 1982). Several

studies have looked at how negative attitudes toward computers can influence the

learning process, and students' attitudes can enhance or hinder knowledge acquisition

(e.g., Griswold, 1983; Koohang, 1987, 1989; Marcoulides, 1989, 1991). Francis (1993)

expounded upon this, saying that "attitudes have long been recognized as important

predictors of individual differences in educational application, learning and achievement"

(p. 251). These facts rarely seem to be considered by many corporate leaders, who instead see the fiscal advantages to technology-enabled learning as opposed to the combination of learning and business advantages (American Management Association, 2003). As Koroghlanian and Brinkerhoff (2000) noted, "In general, research in Internet-delivered instruction has reflected practice rather than driven it" (p. 119).

In addition, the success of any e-learning implementation within a corporate culture is dependent upon a clear understanding of its cultural impact. Harreld (1998) noted that implementing new technologies within a culture that is not prepared to embrace them is useless; the culture needs to be ready in order for success to happen. Hall (2001) echoed this same notion, stating that organizations need to conduct a very thorough needs assessment on the potential roadblocks to success for any type of technology-enabled learning initiative. Rosenberg (2002) noted that there are typically three challenges to implementing a successful e-learning initiative for an organization: (a) motivation of the participants, (b) competence of the participants, and (c) resources for supporting the implementation. Motivation of the participants comes, in part, by conducting a readiness assessment (or performance analysis) of the culture and anticipating why potential learners will resist embracing the technology-enabled learning. As Clark and Sugrue (2001) noted, our "attitudes, beliefs and values influence our motivation to learn" (p. 81). Motivation is our enthusiasm to engage in an undertaking and then the effort put forth to accomplish that undertaking (Clark & Sugrue). Rosenberg's (2002) discussion of competence of the participants focuses on the individual's level of skill and competence to engage in the e-learning environment and initiative. Finally, the last challenge discussed by Rosenberg (2002), resource, refers to the human and technical infrastructure to support the initiative.

The problem facing many corporate training leaders is that they may not have any benchmark data as to employee attitudes towards computers or their self-perceived computer competence. Corporations may invest thousands, if not millions of dollars into technology-enabled learning solutions only to find out that these tools are not used to their fullest extent or provide employees with a negative experience because of their preconceived attitudes toward computers. This lack of use, user dissatisfaction, or low attitude would be attributed to low employee computer knowledge or comfort level with the technology or employees' negative attitudes towards the use of computers. Studies show that an individual's self-reported computer competence is a critical predictor for the use of computer technology (Delcourt & Kinzie, 1993; Jorde-Bloom, 1988; Kinzie, Delcourt, & Powers, 1994). This fact is often overlooked by corporate leadership. In addition, as noted earlier in the literature, in the corporate sector, there is a push to focus instructional delivery methods toward electronic media and away from instructor-led facilitation because of the fiscal advantages this delivery methodology can bring without a true regard for the appropriateness of this media to the audience or learner. While the debate continues between those who believe like Clark (2001) that "media are mere vehicles that deliver instruction but do not influence student achievement" (p. 2) and those who believe media do influence the learning process (Kozma, 2001), there is no question as to the benefits that e-learning has within the corporate sector regarding cost-effectiveness, access to learning modules both synchronously and asynchronously, and more effective use of training resources and, therefore, higher return on investment of certain training expenditures (Rosenberg, 2001; Rossett, 2002; Urban & Weggen, 2000). However, because of the lack of instruments that focus on these phenomena, it is difficult for any organization to benchmark employees' readiness to embrace technology-enabled learning solutions with regard to their self-reported computer competence as well as their attitude toward computers and attitude toward e-learning.

Research Questions to Be Investigated

In this research study, the author investigated eight specific research questions. To do this, the author first created an instrument that measures corporate adult learners' self-reported computer competence as well as their attitude toward computer technology and technology-enabled learning (also defined as e-learning). Next, the author gathered data to support the instrument's overall validity and reliability. With the data gathered from this pilot study complete, the author was able to answer three questions:

1. What is the level of corporate adult learners' attitudes towards computers?

2. What is the level of corporate adult learners' self-perceived levels of computer competence?

3. What is the level of corporate adult learners' attitudes toward technology-enabled learning and training?

Based upon key findings in previous studies, the author also sought to investigate relationships among benchmark corporate adult learners' attitudes toward computer technology, attitude toward technology-enabled learning, and their self-reported computer competence and specific demographic variables collected from the subjects. These five research questions include

1. Is there a correlation between age and self-reported computer literacy?

2. Is there a correlation between age and attitudes toward computers and attitudes toward e-learning?

3. Is there a correlation between educational attainment levels and attitudes toward e-learning?

4. Is there a correlation between gender and attitudes toward computers and attitudes toward e-learning?

5. Is there a correlation between attitudes toward e-learning and experience with various everyday technologies (such as the Internet, automated teller machine, and e-mail)?

Statement of Purpose and Rationale

In this study, the author created a valid and reliable instrument to measure employees' self-reported computer competence, attitudes toward computer technology, and attitudes toward computer-enabled learning (e-learning). Although some instruments exist around two of the phenomena being investigated (computer competence and attitudes toward computers), most of these instruments have been focused toward the kindergarten through Grade 12 (K-12) or American college learning environment with little appropriateness toward the corporate, adult learner. Although studies have shown that self-reported measures may be biased when measuring phenomena that could be classified as "sensitive," such as those involving social issues or criminal disobedience (Edwards, 1957), when the phenomena being examined are not sensitive self-reported measures can be very accurate (Ajzen, 1988; Parry & Crossley, 1950; Pomazal & Jaccard, 1976). In addition, instruments reviewed by the author around the phenomenon of self-reported computer competence or computer literacy tend to be dated in their examination of computer technology (Delcourt & Kinzie, 1993). As technology becomes more pervasive in our society and rapidly grows, past instruments looked at skills such as computer programming as being indicators of success with computer skills, which the author hypothesized is not an accurate indicator of the successful use of technology-enabled learning methods within the 21st century (Kay, 1993b; Woodrow, 1992).

In addition, instruments that purport to measure attitudes toward computers do not specifically address subjects' attitudes or experience with using technology-enabled learning methods or e-learning, an ever-increasing component of the corporate learning landscape (Rosenberg, 2001; Rossett, 2002; Urban & Weggen, 2000). Conflicting reports have been discovered around the impact that gender has on attitudes toward computers; some note that females are more anxious than males (e.g., Griswold, 1983; Koohang, 1986; Loyd & Gressard, 1986), while other studies did not find significant differences in males and female attitude toward computers or computer literacy (e.g. Heissen, Glass, & Knight, 1987; Woodrow, 1992, 1994). These conflicting results provide an opportunity to explore gender differences further within the phenomena of attitudes toward computers, computer literacy, and attitudes toward e-learning.

Once a valid and reliable instrument has been developed that purports to measure these three phenomena, the data garnered from the instrument could then be used in a variety of ways. Instructional designers and training management could use the data to develop treatments for their corporate adult learners to help improve their basic computer utilization skills or to develop interventions to modify the learners' attitudes toward technology-enabled learning. Organizations could also use the newly developed instrument to conduct a benchmark performance analysis to ascertain whether or not their particular business environment's employees are truly ready for the company to incorporate e-learning strategies into its training and development delivery methodology. In addition, businesses could use the instrument once an employee is hired within an organization to ascertain if the new employee would be best suited to participate in future training efforts that are technology enabled or if these learning events should be conducted in a more traditional instructor-led format that best meets the needs of the learner. Again, while some argue that the instructional delivery methodology should not matter regarding the transfer of knowledge (Clark, 2001), it should be up to the individual learning organization to determine the best method of delivery of its content, weighing the variables of learner preference and fiscal benefits.

Objectives

The primary objective of the research study was to create a reliable and valid instrument that will measure employee attitudes toward computer technology, attitudes and experience with e-learning, and their self-reported computer competence that is appropriate for the adult learner in today's corporate setting. A tertiary objective of this study was to analyze the data from the pilot group to explore certain correlations between the variables collected from the newly created instrument and the demographic variables of the participants.

Through the accomplishment of these two objectives, the author hopes to provide an expansion of knowledge to the field by developing a valid, reliable, and concise instrument to use for future performance analysis looking at these phenomena that can determine an organization's readiness to venture into e-learning and technology-enabled learning from the learners' perspective. Unlike previous instruments developed specifically for a K-12 or college student audience, this instrument would be appropriate for use on an adult subject within the corporate environment.

Elements, Hypotheses, and Theories to Be Investigated

The research study examined the development of an instrument to measure subjects' attitudes toward computers, attitudes toward e-learning, and self-reported computer competence. An analysis of the pilot study data was also done to explore relationships between attitudes toward computers, attitudes toward e-learning, self-reported computer competence, and demographic variables (such as age, gender, and level of education and current technology use). The author investigated six hypotheses during the development of this new instrument:

1. Subjects' attitudes toward computers will be positively correlated with their attitude toward e-learning as a method of learning.

2. Subjects' age will be negatively correlated with self-reported computer competence.

3. Subjects' age will be negatively correlated with attitudes toward e-learning.

4. Subjects' level of education will be positively correlated with their attitudes toward e-learning.

5. Subjects' self-reported computer competence will be positively correlated with overall attitudes toward e-learning.

6. There will be no significant difference between gender and attitudes toward computers, attitudes toward technology-enabled learning, and self-reported computer competence.

Limitations of the Study

Although the newly developed instrument being developed will have a broad use, there are limits to its utilization. First, the instrument was developed for use by corporate, adult learners and may not be appropriate for use with other populations, such as the K-12 students, traditional-aged college students, or adults working in a noncorporate organization (such as academia). Although it was the author's goal to develop a universally acceptable instrument for succinctly measuring computer attitude, attitudes toward e-learning, and self-reported computer competence, it was beyond the scope of this study to validate and test the reliability of the instrument on nonadult, noncorporate learners.

The pilot study was conducted on a certain group of North American business personnel, and a second limitation is using the instrument beyond a North American audience. It was beyond the scope of this research study to determine if the newly developed instrument was valid and reliable to other non-North American audiences (such as Asian, European, or South American audiences).

Finally, the technological advances within our society have rapidly changed over the past few years, greatly impacting the way we live and how we learn. Like other instruments developed that focus on the measurement of computer literacy or competence as well as attitudes toward computer technology, there is a limited "shelf life" around this type of measurement due to the rapid advances of technology. An additional limitation to this study would be the potential limited time usage that the instrument could be employed. Although the author believes the phenomenon of attitudes toward computers is less impacted by specific computer advances, self-reported computer competence is contingent upon the current technological trends, and e-learning methodology being utilized today (and measured in the newly-developed instrument) may be obsolete tomorrow. Like other instruments before that have attempted to measure computer competence, technological advances could make the facet of the instrument focused on self-reported computer competence quickly out of date, making it necessary to update and revalidate the instrument as new questions more appropriate to current technology trends are incorporated into the instrument.

Definition of Terms

For the purposes of this study, the author defined key terms associated with the phenomena being examined. They include the following:

1. Aptitude is the characteristics of a person that forecasts his or her probability of success under a given treatment (Cronbach & Snow, 1969).

2. Computer anxiety is "the complex emotional reactions that are evoked in individuals who interpret computers as personally threatening" (Raub, 1981, p. 14).

3. Computer confidence is "related to the confidence in the ability to learn about or use computers" (Loyd & Gressard, 1984, p. 303).

4. Computer liking is the "enjoyment or liking of computers and using computers" (Loyd & Gressard, 1984, p. 303).

5. Computer literacy is "whatever a person needs to know and do with computers in order to function competently in our information-based society" (National Center for Education Statistics, 1983, p. 8).

6. Computer usefulness is "consisting of the perception of computers as helpful in one's future work" (Loyd & Gressard, 1984, p. 303).

7. Computerphobia is "a person's anxiety and fear about computers" (Koohang, 1986, p. 1).

8. Corporate adult learner is a person over 18 years of age who is employed part- or full-time within a nonacademic setting. This could be an organization within the public sector (such as a nonprofit organization) or the private sector (such as a business).

9. e-Learning is also referred to as *technology-enabled learning*. It is the use of such electronic media as CD-ROM, the Internet, private intranet, or any combination of these in order to facilitate training and education (Commission on Technology and Adult Learning, 2000; Urban & Weggen, 2000).

10. Performance analysis is defined as

the process for partnering with clients to help them define and achieve their goals.

It involves reaching out for several perspectives on a problem or opportunity, determining any and all drivers toward or barriers to successful performance, and proposing a solution system based on what is learned, not on what is typically done. (Rossett, 1999, p. 13)

11. Self-efficacy is "personal judgment of one's capability to organize and implement actions in specific situations that may contain novel, unpredictable, and possible stressful features" (Schunk, 1984, p. 49). In terms of *computer self-efficacy*, this then is the personal judgment of one's capability to use a computer effectively (also referred to as computer competence or computer literacy).

Chapter Summary

The corporate sector is quickly embracing e-learning and technology-enabled learning to accomplish many of its training and learning objectives. However, the problem exists that many corporations are delving into technology-enabled learning without understanding their end user's computer competence or attitude; they are simply launching e-learning efforts without determining if an e-learning solution is right for a particular business environment from a learners' perspective. In addition, although there exists several instruments that measure attitudes toward computers and self-reported computer competence, most are focused on the American academic or K-12 learner and may not have applicability to the corporate, adult learner in the early 21st century. Few instruments exist that are applicable to the corporate adult learner that specifically address attitudes toward technology-enabled learning or e-learning.

This research study focused on the creation of a valid, reliable, and concise instrument that measures employees' self-reported computer competence, overall attitudes toward computer technology, and attitudes toward technology-enabled learning (or e-learning). Through the validation and reliability analysis, the newly developed instrument is applicable for use with the adult, corporate learner as opposed to existing instruments that are aimed more toward the academic setting. In addition, the research study explored relationships between the data provided in the newly created instrument and certain demographic variables of the participants in the study.

Limitations exist to this study. As noted earlier, the instrument developed is for use by corporate, adult learners and may not be appropriate for usage with populations such as K-12 students, college students, or adults working within an academic environment. The pilot study was conducted on a group of North American business personnel, and a secondary limitation of the study is its use beyond a North American audience. Finally, like other instruments developed that focus on the measurement of attitudes toward computer technology, there is a limited shelf life around this type of measurement due to the rapid advances of technology within our information-based society.

Chapter 2: Review of the Literature

Historical Overview of the Theory and Research Literature

The phenomena of attitudes toward computers and computer literacy are not new concepts being examined within the past few years; conversely, many researchers have looked at these phenomena for decades. Today, however, the importance of computer literacy cannot be underestimated given the relevance of computers in modern society and specifically within business and education. As M. Jones and Pearson (1996) noted, "computer literacy is necessary in today's business world, not just for survival, but for basic functioning" (p. 17). The progression of this particular body of knowledge stems from several foundational constructs associated with anxiety and attitude and their impact on learning. Francis (1993) expounded upon this, saying that "attitudes have long been recognized as important predictors of individual differences in educational application, learning and achievement" (p. 251).

Specifically, theories around self-efficacy and attitudes toward mathematics provide the foundation for exploration within the phenomena of attitudes toward computers. *Attitude toward computers* emerged as having two varying definitions in the literature: (a) as defined by anxiety only and (b) with an expanded definition to include anxiety and other dimensions of attitude. This research, in turn, provides the foundation for the exploration of the phenomena of attitudes toward e-learning. In addition, early research around end-user attitudes toward computer applications also provides a basis with which to explore students' attitudes toward applications used for teaching and learning or e-learning. Computer literacy had been explored since early attempts to define the term were created in the 1970s as microcomputers began to emerge in the United States school system and business environments. Interwoven among all these studies are results around certain demographic relationships and attitudes toward computers and attitudes toward e-learning, providing a foundation with which to analyze current relationships among demographics variables and the phenomena being examined in the research study.

First, this review of the literature explores the basic concepts around self-efficacy and foundational works around mathematics anxiety and how these two phenomena relate to the construct of computer anxiety. Then the review of the literature chronologically examines the relevant literature around the phenomena of computer anxiety and computer literacy, followed by a review of the literature that simultaneously examined these two phenomena. Finally, the review of the literature looks at the relevant literature regarding the phenomena of attitudes toward e-learning, first starting with earlier research around attitudes toward computer applications and then relevant literature studies around the phenomena of attitudes toward multimedia instruction. The ways in which researchers created their respective instruments and their steps to establish the instruments' overall reliability and validity are also discussed within each of these sections. Finally, a discussion of the trends and major contributions the literature has on the phenomena being investigated by this research study as well as the development of an instrument of measurement for the phenomena to be examined is presented.

Understanding of Self-Efficacy

The concept of self-efficacy provides one of the strongest foundations for the phenomenon of attitudes in general. As noted earlier, Bandura (1977) defined this concept around the notion that an individual who judges him or herself as being competent to perform a certain task (or efficacious) will tend to attempt and succeed in those tasks. Bandura (as cited in Murphy, Coover, & Owen ,1988) noted that there are four ways in which an individual determines his or her competence in being able to perform a task: (a) performance accomplishment, (b) vicarious learning experiences, (c) verbal persuasion, and (d) affective arousal. An individual gathers data through these four filters and appraises his or her individual ability to do a task. This, in turn, will help determine the individual's success or failure at a task. Bandura (as cited in Murphy et al.) stated, "Research has shown that self-percepts of efficacy influence choice of activities and environmental settings, effort expenditure, and persistence regardless of whether such appraisals are faulty or accurate" (p. 4). Schunk (1984) defined self-efficacy as "personal judgment of one's capability to organize and implement actions in specific situations that may contain novel, unpredictable, and possible stressful features" (p. 49). In terms of computer self-efficacy, this then is the personal judgment of one's capability to use a computer effectively (also referred to as computer competence or computer literacy; Delcourt & Kinzie, 1993; Milbrath & Kinzie, 2000; Moroz & Nash, 1997a; Murphy et al.). Therefore, if a student judges him or herself as being competent with computers, he or she will be competent with computers (Woodrow, 1987).

Measures for Attitude Toward Mathematics

It has been documented that mathematical skills are positively related to computer programming ability (Howell, Vincent, & Gay, 1967), and therefore, much of the research done with regard to measuring attitudes toward computers originated from the work done around the measurement of attitudes toward mathematics. Fennema and Sherman (1976) were early pioneers in this area, and using a grant from the National Science Foundation, they developed nine instruments that looked into various domains of mathematics in education. Although Fennema and Sherman developed these nine instruments that looked at various aspects of mathematics anxiety (called the Fennema-

Sherman Mathematics Attitude Scales), three of these scales developed reflect some of the earlier works done by researchers around computer attitudes. These include (a) the Attitudes Toward Success in Mathematics Scale, which is designed to measure the degree to which students anticipate positive or negative consequences as a result of success in mathematics; (b) the Confidence in Learning Mathematics Scale reports to measure confidence in one's ability to learn and perform well on mathematical tasks; and (c) the Mathematics Anxiety Scale reports to measure feelings of anxiety, dread, nervousness, and associated bodily symptoms related to doing mathematics. The authors conducted two empirical studies in 1975 (where $N = 1,233$ with American students in Grades 9 through 12) and 1976 (where $N = 1,500$ with American students in Grades 6 through 8). One of the authors' main goals was to determine if gender made a difference in the various attitudes toward mathematics, and in subsequent studies, they found that, when both females and males study the same amount of mathematics, differences in learning mathematics are minimal; significantly fewer females elect to study mathematics, and this, therefore, creates a lack of mathematic knowledge and comfort (Fennema, 1977). This study was the beginning of many that looked at gender differences in mathematics anxiety and achievement.

Two additional researchers examined how independent variables correlated with mathematics anxiety. Using a slightly modified version of the Fennema-Sherman Mathematics Attitude Scales (Fennema & Sherman, 1976), Chisholm (1980) analyzed the avoidance of mathematics by a heterogeneous subject base. The data from this study suggest that five variables can help predict mathematic avoidance: (a) the subject's problem-solving mind-set, (b) the subject's self-confidence in learning mathematics, (c) the subject's perception of the usefulness of mathematics, (d) the subject's overall anxiety toward mathematics, and (e) factors relating to the subject's father. As this review of the literature shows, variables of self-confidence, perception of usefulness, and anxiety are variables researched in computer anxiety. Calvert (1981) looked at college students' math anxiety and four independent variables: gender, age, highest level of math course previously completed, and the last grade received in a mathematics course. A study involving 441 students enrolled in precalculus mathematics courses was conducted to measure the correlation. Calvert used the Mathematics Anxiety Rating Scale (MARS) to measure their math anxiety. The data suggested that all independent variables except for age were statistically significant in the determination of math anxiety level; female college students were significantly more likely to have higher levels of math anxiety than males, and students who only completed a general mathematics course were more likely to have higher levels of math anxiety than students who had completed more difficult math courses. These variables have also been explored with regard to computer anxiety and achievement with significant emphasis placed on the analysis of gender issues and computer anxiety (Koohang, 1987, 1989).

These studies are but a small sample of the multitude of research conducted around the phenomena of mathematics anxiety showing a correlation between experience and levels of anxiety. This correlation provides a fundamental concept that was explored in the domain of computer anxiety and experience.

Measures for Attitude Toward Computers

As personal computers became standard fixtures in American schools, some researchers began to inquire about the impact of these machines on student performance. Realizing that placing computers in the classroom "could be a waste of time and money if proper curricula and laboratory experiences do not support the development of positive attitudes toward using these machines to facilitate learning" (Reece & Gable, 1982, p. 913); several authors began to measure the phenomenon of "attitude toward computers." Like the research done around math anxiety and self-efficacy, researchers hypothesized that a direct link existed between students' anxiety toward the subject of computers and their success, and wanted to explore measuring that phenomena (Bear, 1990; Loyd & Gressard, 1984; Murphy et al., 1988).

Attitude defined as anxiety only. In early studies and instruments created to measure attitude toward computers, the term attitude was limited to the dimension of anxiety. Raub (1981) defined computer anxiety as "the complex emotional reactions that are evoked in individuals who interpret computers as personally threatening" (p. 14). Like the studies done around mathematics and the limits that anxiety can have on performance in a certain domain, the degree to which computers can be used effectively can be influenced by computer anxiety. "The higher the level of computer anxiety, the lower the computer achievement" (Marcoulides, Mayes, & Wiseman, 1995, p. 805).

One of the first groups to study this phenomenon, Simonson, Maurer, Montag-Torardi, and Whitaker (1987) looked at what exactly computer literacy and computer anxiety are in their study. Their ultimate research goal was to develop a standardized test to measure computer literacy. They first defined computer literacy to include four dimensions: (a) computer attitudes, (b) computer applications, (c) computer systems, and (d) computer programming. Although computer applications, computer systems, and computer programming are related to direct computer experience, it was important for the authors to create a measure of computer anxiety so that "of the attitudinal competencies identified . . . those related to apprehension, or fear, felt by a person toward computers was considered the most critical for development as part of this project" (Simonson et al.,

p. 238). They created an instrument called the Computer Anxiety Index (CAIN), first identifying a large number of items that described people's anxiety toward computers, which was followed by a pilot test to determine which items discriminated the phenomenon best. This was repeated until the 26-item instrument was developed with data collected from its pilot testing revealing a reliability estimate of 0.94 using Chronbach's alpha (Simonson et al.). The authors then administered the CAIN and, using a test-retest scenario, determined its reliability to be approximately 0.90.

Simonson et al. (1987) chose to identify its concurrent validity of the CAIN instrument with the State-Trait Anxiety Inventory (STAI), an instrument developed by Spielberger, Gorsuch, and Lushene (1970), which is an instrument designed to measure general anxiety and not specifically to measure computer anxiety but whose validity had been documented in many previous research studies (Simonson et al.). In addition, they collected observable anxiety traits among the students participating in the pilot study. "The three scores, CAIN, STAI, and the observed anxiety ratings, were correlated. The CAIN was found to correlate significantly to both the STAI and the observation score (r = 0.32 and 0.36 respectively)" (Simonson et al., p. 240). In addition, a normative data-collection process for the CAIN was conducted, resulting in data from 1,943 students in a variety of academic settings (junior high to college). Sixty-seven of these students also completed the Standardized Test for Computer Literacy also by Simonson et al. The important discovery within this data set was the negative correlation between computer literacy and anxiety, but the authors noted that more exploration between this relationship should be investigated.

Heinssen et al. (1987) were also exploring attitudes using the anxiety-only perspective. Heinssen et al. developed and validated the Computer Anxiety Rating Scale

(CARS), a 20-item, Likert scale instrument that purports to measure the behavioral, cognitive, and affective components of computer anxiety. The authors first interviewed individuals who considered themselves computer anxious and those having no computer anxiety in order to generate a pool of items for the instrument (yielding $n = 26$). This list was then reviewed by content experts who rated the statements' perceived level of anxiety and eliminated 6 items. Their sample included 270 college students (103 men and 168 women), and they were given the CARS instrument as well as the Computer Experience Questionnaire (developed by the authors) and the Computer Attitude Scale (CAS) by Loyd and Gressard (1984); these were administered to help establish the CARS' concurrent validity. To establish the instrument's discriminant validity, the authors administered the 40-item Math Anxiety Rating Scale (Richardson & Woolfolk, 1980) and the 37-item Test Anxiety Scale (Sarason, 1978). The authors concluded that higher computer anxiety was associated with math and test anxiety as well as lower computer experience. It is important to note that Heinssen et al. find any correlation to computer anxiety and gender.

Another attempt to create a measure of computer anxiety was attempted by Marcoulides (1989), who created the CAS to measure students' anxiety toward computers. Specifically, the author looked at two factors associated with computer anxiety: (1) general attitudes toward computers; and (2) equipment anxiety. The author determined the instrument's construct validity through the use of subject-matter experts; followed by a pilot test on a sample of 225 college students. Marcoulides (1989) determined the CAS to be reliable by performing a test-retest scenario with a coefficient of 0.77. The author further validated the instrument through intercorrelational analysis of the instrument's items. The CAS was then used in a secondary study by Marcoulides

(1991) to analyze the attitudes and reactions to two populations of students: one in the United States and the other in the People's Republic of China. The goal of this study was to examine the comparability of the construct of computer anxiety across the two different cultures specifically answering the research question, "do students in the United States differ from students in the People's Republic of China in their attitudes and reactions toward computers?" (Marcoulides, 1991, p. 282). The author found that the two factors being measured in the CAS–general computer anxiety and anxiety toward computer equipment (such as the computer itself, a printer, etc.)–did not differ significantly between American and Chinese cultures. This study proved to be a good baseline study to explore computer anxiety in non-U.S. populations, and it was one of the first attempts by a researcher to conduct comparative analysis between cultures within the phenomenon of computer anxiety.

Research in computer anxiety overall focused on the population of students, and Marcoulides et al. (1995) noted the lack of studies done on the corporate sector, saying, "unfortunately, most of the computer anxiety research conducted to date has focused on samples from the same population, namely, American undergraduate college students . . . Little is known about the attitudes and perceptions of individuals in the workforce" (pp. 805-806). To that point, they looked at computer anxiety within the corporate setting, specifically members of a law enforcement agency. Using the 20-item CAS, the authors gathered data from two groups: 320 participants from law enforcement and 258 college students. Both groups were given a test-retest scenario for the CAS instrument, similar to the process conducted in Marcoulides' 1991 study. Comparing the results from the two groups, there was consistency among the construct of computer anxiety, suggesting that the CAS instrument is capable of measuring the same anxiety constructs for a variety of groups. It is important to note that this was one of the first attempts to look at the construct of computer anxiety among adults within the corporate sector; and through its continued use, the CAS was noted by Marcoulides et al. to be "an invaluable tool for researchers and practitioners interested in computer anxiety and its effect on the workforce" (p. 809). Unfortunately, as the authors noted, the very homogeneous population (320 law enforcement professionals) did not necessarily afford generalizable results to other corporate populations.

Some researchers have commented that there is a lack of consistency with the definition of the phenomena computer anxiety. McInerney, Marsh, and McInerney (1999) attempted to design a scale that would "clearly explicate these dimensions [of computer anxiety] and that would be sure, via valid and reliable scores, the multiple dimensions of computer anxiety in a training situation for adult learners" (pp. 451-452). Taking a qualitative research methodology as the basis for their instrument development, McInerney et al. conducted interviews and focus groups in order to identify the underlying negative cognitions and anxiety with regard to learning to use computers. The researchers used a sample of 794 Australian undergraduate (adult) students from two different institutions, but they were from a variety of ethnographic backgrounds (Australian, Chinese, Greek, Italian, Spanish, Arabic, Croatian, Lebanese, and Vietnamese). They developed a 65-item instrument divided into four subscales: (a) gaining initial computing skills, (b) sense of control, (c) computing self-concept, and (d) state of anxiety in computing situations. After conducting multimethod research techniques, including factor analysis, the authors concluded that the Computer Anxiety and Learning Measure was indeed reliable and valid instrument among the sample population. The importance of this experience was twofold: (a) they attempted to focus on one facet of attitude toward computers: anxiety, and (b) the authors explored non-U.S. subjects within their research.

To summarize, in early studies and instruments created to measure attitudes toward computers, the term attitude was limited to the dimension of anxiety. Simonson et al. (1987) were among the first group to look at the phenomena through the creation and validation of a newly developed instrument to measure the phenomena; the important discovery within this data set was the negative correlation between computer literacy and anxiety. Heinssen et al. (1987) similarly developed and validated another instrument purported to measure computer anxiety, and like Simonson et al., they concluded that higher computer anxiety was associated with math and test anxiety as well as lower computer experience. The authors of this particular study did not find any correlation to computer anxiety and gender. Marcoulides (1989) created an instrument to measure students' anxiety toward computers and took several tactics to support overall validity of the instrument. In addition to this initial pilot study, Marcoulides (1991) further validated the instrument in a subsequent study and found that general computer anxiety and anxiety toward computer equipment did not differ significantly between American and Chinese college students. Marcoulides et al. (1995) then studied computer anxiety within a nonacademic setting: members of a law enforcement agency. They found that their instrument was capable of measuring the same anxiety constructs for both college students and adults working within the law enforcement field, but although this was one of the first studies to look at a nonacademic population, the results were not generalizable due to the homogeneity of the population. Finally, McInerney et al. (1999) took a qualitative research approach to measuring the phenomena of computer anxiety. The importance of this experience was twofold: they attempted to focus on one facet of attitude toward computers: anxiety, and the authors explored non-U.S. subjects within their research.

Attitude definition broadened beyond anxiety. As research progressed in the area of identifying and measuring attitudes toward computers, researchers expanded their definition of attitude beyond the limited definition of just anxiety although, in most examinations, anxiety remained a facet of attitude. Francis (1993) argued that, in the field of attitude research, great debate exists around what the term attitude means. One facet claims that attitude is comprised of three areas: affective, behavioral, and cognitive, while others focus only the affective domain. Francis argued that this lack of clarity has led to a variety of instruments intended to measure attitude toward computers but with varying definitions of what attitude means.

Early investigations into the phenomena of attitude. The researchers who were among the first to look at an expanded definition of attitude toward computers beyond the definition of anxiety were Stevens (1980, 1982), Raub (1981), Reece and Gable (1982), and Griswold (1983). Stevens (1980) noted an early need to measure knowledge levels and attitudes toward computers of (a) college students (preservice teachers), (b) current K-12 teachers, and (c) teacher faculty in the state of Nebraska. Raub noted that, among adults (defined as those above the age of 20) who are confronted with new technologies, you will often find indifference, negative attitudes, or computer anxiety. To measure attitude and anxiety, the author developed the Computers in Education Survey, a brief, seven-question Likert-scale survey examining attitudes toward the use of computers in education and society overall, and a modified version of the Minnesota Computer Literacy and Awareness Assessment (Anderson, Krohn, & Sandman, 1980). Stevens' findings suggest that all three responder subgroups strongly favored instruction to foster computer literacy among secondary schools, but responders did not feel knowledgeable enough to teach computer literacy learning events. Interestingly, Stevens found that the subgroup of student teachers was the most reserved regarding the use of computers as instructional tools. The author then used the data collected in this survey to create treatments to assist educators at all levels to use computers as instructional tools (Stevens, 1980).

Griswold (1983) acknowledged this work done by Stevens (1980) but criticized the results as being "based upon low survey return rates" (p. 92). Griswold noted that there tends to be a resistance among teachers to the use of computer technology and hypothesized that it had to do with their limited computer literacy. The author further hypothesized that computer application skills are needed in order to enhance computer literacy. Griswold examined three hypotheses using a 20-item questionnaire created by the author: (a) that locus of control which "describes the generalized expectancy about how reinforcement is controlled i.e. by internal or external means" (p. 93), accounts for greater computer awareness than other variables such as age, gender, or math skills; (b) that two independent variables of males and those more inclined for math skills tend to have greater computer awareness than females and those with lower math skills; and (c) that younger individuals tend to be more aware of computer applications than older individuals. Griswold concluded that the data collected from the 119 students supported Hypothesis 1 and Hypothesis 2; but Hypothesis 3 was rejected; this discovery was very unexpected. Griswold concluded that "for society to become computer literate, we must insure that teachers recognize the importance of computers and their applications" (p. 99).

In a replicated study, Stevens (1982) set out to see if increases in computer knowledge and attitude changed for K-12 teachers, student teachers, and teacher educators in the state of Nebraska. Using the Computers in Education instruments first developed by the author (Stevens, 1980), this study looked at comparable sample size populations from the 1979 study and analyzed the results using a one-way analysis of variance to determine significant changes. The author found that between 2 years a significant increase in knowledge about computers occurred with the representative samples but did not find any significant changes in attitudes toward computers between the two studies.

To further build upon Stevens' (1982) research, Woodrow (1987) conducted a replicate study to benchmark teachers' attitudes toward computer technology. She noted the importance of this effort in the early adoption of computers in education:

> The role of teacher attitudes towards computers is so important to the successful implementation of computers in education that the attitudes of the educators involved should be evaluated both prior to, as well as periodically during the early stages of their introduction. Based upon such evaluations, pre-service and inservice courses can be designed to effect the change with the greatest efficiency. (p. 27)

Using a modified version of the Computers in Education Questionnaire (Stevens, 1980), Woodrow (1987) wanted to compare the instrument's results by administering it to 58 teachers and 89 student teachers who were determined to already have a positive attitude toward computers for educational use. The results were then compared to the 1981 study by Stevens using the same instrument. Findings showed that the 1985 groups (measured by Woodrow, 1987) were more positive about computers in education than the 1981 group originally analyzed by Stevens (1982). Both groups agreed that there was a growing importance for computer education and the improvement of computer competence among high school students, and based upon these findings, Woodrow advocated both inservice courses for current teachers on computer literacy as well as set curricula around computer technology for preservice teachers. In addition to her conclusions, Woodrow's (1987) research further validated the results obtained by Stevens (1980) and the Computers in Education Questionnaire instrument.

Like Stevens (1980, 1982), Raub (1981) examined three related factors of computer anxiety: (a) what attitudes do college students possess regarding computers that cause them anxiety, (b) what variables correlate to computer anxiety, and (c) to what extent does computer experience diminish computer anxiety? Raub developed the Attitudes Toward Computers questionnaire and administered the instrument to 220 American undergraduate students. The author analyzed students' results of the instrument over two semesters in two introductory computer programming classes and one introductory psychology class. A reduction in anxiety toward computers was examined by comparing the changes in attitude toward computers between the semesters. Analysis discovered five independent variables to be significant contributors to computer anxiety: gender, level of computer experience, college major, math anxiety, and trait anxiety. Although gender overall was a variable related to computer anxiety, further analysis revealed different combinations of predictor variables. Based upon these data, Raub concluded that computer attitudes are gender specific and culturally learned and that programming courses reduced anxiety toward computers.

Also expanding the definition of attitude toward computers beyond the dimension of anxiety, Reece and Gable (1982) developed and validated their own instrument, entitled Attitude Toward Computers (not to be confused with the Attitude Toward

Computers instrument developed by Raub in 1981). First, they defined attitude as being comprised of three components (affective, behavioral, and cognitive) and developed their instrument with the assistance of subject-matter experts to establish the instrument's content validity. This resulted in a 30-item instrument then distributed to a pilot group of 233 American seventh- and eighth-grade students; analysis of these data helped confirm the instrument's construct validity, with an internal consistency reliability estimate of 0.87. Reece and Gable concluded that the instrument was indeed reliable and valid in determining students' attitudes toward computers in the three domains of attitude: affective, behavioral, and cognitive. However, one of the challenges with the Reece and Gable examination of attitudes toward computers was their limited subject demographics (seventh- and eighth-grade American students). In addition, other researchers criticized their findings; Bear, Richards, and Lancaster (1987) noted that "these researchers provided no evidence for the external validity of their instrument" (p. 208).

Development and use of the Bath County Computer Attitudes Scale (BCCAS).
Bear et al. (1987) developed one of the more widely used scales to measure attitudes toward computers: the BCCAS. The 38 Likert items were designed to assess attitudes toward five domains of attitude: (a) general computer use, (b) computer-assisted instruction, (c) programming and technical concepts, (d) social issues surrounding computer use, and (e) computer history. The authors pilot tested their scale on 398 rural western Virginia, United States, students in Grades 4 through 12, and the instrument was found to be valid and reliable in the measurement of the five domains noted above. However, the authors sought to reduce the number of items but retain the same level of validity and reliability so they examined the 26 items with the highest corrected item-to-total correlations. The internal consistency (alpha coefficient) of these 26 items was 0.94,

equal with the original 36-item instrument. This revised version was then administered to 551 students with similar demographics as the initial pilot, and the scores were found to be predictably related to computer experience and usage, educational and career plans, choice of favorite school subject, and attitudes toward school subjects. Overall, the data supported that the revised 26-item instrument of the BCCAS was indeed valid as a measure of attitudes toward computers.

Because of the perceived reliability and validity of the BCCAS, other researchers sought to use the instrument to measure attitudes toward computers but on different populations. Pike, Hofner, and Erlank (1993) conducted a study on 462 students in western South Africa with results indicating that students who were leaving school to pursue work in the computer field had more positive attitudes toward computers than other students leaving school, supporting the overall construct validity of the BCCAS. Miller and Varma (1993) used the BCCAS on 279 Grade 6 and 7 students in Dehru Dun, India. They report that variables, such as computer experiences, computer usage, and mathematics anxiety, were significant factors in determining overall attitude toward computers. Francis and Evans (1995) measured attitude towards computers among 378 Welsh college students. The authors explored the concurrent validity of the BCCAS with four other instruments purported to measure attitude toward computers (Gressard & Loyd, 1985; Griswold, 1983; Reece & Gable, 1982; Stevens, 1980), with correlations ranging between 0.61 and 0.91, but the author interpreted the results as strong supportive evidence to the validity of all these scales.

In the first attempt to use the BCCAS in a different language than what it was originally developed, Katz, Evans, and Francis (1995) translated the BCCAS instrument into Hebrew and administered it to 339 undergraduate students in Israel. Although the authors noted that the generalizability of the study is limited (because it was only conducted on one class of undergraduates at one Israeli university), it clearly supports the overall validity and reliability of the instrument. Having administered the BCCAS to 644 Lebanese students in Grades 6 to 12, Yaghi (1997) came to the same conclusion: the BCCAS is a valid and reliable instrument to use in measuring attitude toward computers. To summarize, through these various research examinations, the validity and reliability of the BCCAS was reinforced among a multitude of worldwide student populations: American, South African, Indian, Welsh, and Israeli; however, to date, no exploration of the BCCAS and it applicability to nonacademic settings in the United States or any other country has been conducted.

Similar to Pike et al. (1993), Miller and Varma (1993), Francis and Evans (1995), Katz et al. (1995), and Yaghi (1997), Leutner and Weinsier (1994) set out to validate an existing instrument against a non-American audience. The authors of this study were examining the Computer and Information Technology Attitude Inventory, developed by the authors, to see whether there are differences in attitudes toward computers between students in Europe and the United States. Leutner and Weinsier hypothesized that, because computer usage proliferated in the United States 5 to 10 years before it did in Europe, American students "would have had more contact with computers and information technology, thereby reducing the computer's significance as a controversial theme and an attitude object which affects students' study interests" (p. 571). The Computer and Information Technology Attitude Inventory was administered to 529 students from universities in Belgium, Germany, and the United States. Although the data showed high similarities of the interitem correlation structures across the three samples, some intercultural differences were found. For example, European students have a strong preference for noncomputer courses as opposed to computer courses, while American students do not have a preference.

A repeated theme among many researchers looking at the phenomena of attitudes toward computer is the lack of consistent definition with the term attitudes toward computers. Kay (1993a) noted that the research regarding computer attitude has made it challenging to interpret and compare results from the studies and the varied constructs used to define attitude further complicate the issue. To this end, the author had two research goals in mind with regard to analyzing attitudes toward computers: (a) explore an alternative computer attitude measure based on four constructs developed from general attitude research and (b) investigate the effect of context within this framework. Using a modified version of the Computer Attitude Measure (CAM) initially developed by Kay (1989), the 50-question instrument was administered to 647 preservice teachers in Canada and, similar to Reece and Gable (1982), focused on three constructs of attitude, cognitive, affective, and behavioral, with the addition of analyzing participants' perceived control. Although the author noted that the sample's demographic makeup should be understood (predominantly female, rural, and preservice teachers), the results of the study indicate that "promising statistical results of the student suggest that the four-dimension model may be one way to reorganize and assess the multitude of constructs already identified by computer attitude research" (p. 371).

Development and use of the CAS. In the literature, with the exception of the BCCAS by Bear et al. (1987), few instruments have had as extensive usage as the CAS by Loyd and Gressard (1984). Based upon learning that anxiety toward a given subject could affect learning outcomes (Fennema & Sherman, 1976), Loyd and Gressard (1984) developed and validated their own instrument out of a need to understand students' attitudes toward computers in order to ensure their success in the classroom. They developed the CAS with three subscales--(a) computer liking, (b) computer confidence, and (c) computer anxiety--and set out to provide information on the reliability and factorial validity of the scales used. The authors selected 30 items for their instrument, 10 each from the three domains of attitude (affective, behavioral, and cognitive). Their data suggest that the three subscales are independently reliable and can be used separately (depending on the desired attitudinal domain being analyzed) and the overall score represents general attitudes toward computers. In conclusion, the most important finding in their examination was that, for the high school and college students surveyed, there was a significant relationship between the amount of computer experience and the attitudes toward computers of the subjects with more computer experience corresponding to more positive computer attitudes (Loyd & Gressard, 1984). Also through this research Loyd and Gressard developed one of the most widely used measures of attitudes toward computers to date (Woodrow, 1991).

The population of students was further explored by Koohang (1986), who sought to measure computer anxiety among American high school students in order to determine the relationship between computer anxiety and other variables such as grade level, gender, and previous computer experience. Using the CAS (Loyd & Gressard, 1984), the author found that, whereas grade level was not significant enough to predict computer anxiety or "computerphobia," gender was a significant factor to computer anxiety (males tended to be less anxious about computers than females). In addition, Koohang found that the more computer experience, the less computer anxiety. This study further validated the CAS instrument among its initial target audience: American high school students.

Seven years after the original research, Pope-Davis and Twig (1991) conducted a replicate study originally done by Loyd and Gressard (1984) to examine the affects that age, gender, and computer experience had on attitudes toward computers. Using the CAS (Loyd & Gressard, 1984), the authors implemented a 40-item instrument to measure the 207 college students' attitude toward computers on four subscales: (a) computer anxiety, (b) computer confidence, (c) computer liking, and (d) computer usefulness. They also surveyed demographic data from the subjects in an instrument created by the authors. Contrary to what Koohang (1986) discovered, Pope-Davis and Twig concluded that gender did not have a significant influence in computer attitudes as previous studies have determined. However, the authors found that age did significantly influence attitude toward computers. Computer experience was a significant factor only on the liking subscale and not the other subscales as other studies have found. Overall, the participants of the study were generally positive toward their attitude toward computers, as shown with the average score of the four subscales being 32.97 on a 40-point scale.

Bear et al. (1987) commented that the CAS by Loyd and Gressard (1984) had much promise, but "considerably more research needs to be done to properly document the external validity of their instrument" (p. 208). To help establish the instrument's external validity, Loyd and Loyd (1985) sought to use the instrument on a different target audience than high school or college students: teachers. They hypothesized that, with the increased use of computers in education, teachers' attitudes toward these computers in schools could enhance or hinder the successful use of computers. Specifically, the purpose of their study was (a) to obtain estimates of the reliability of the four subscales of the CAS, (b) to gain information concerning the factorial validity of the subscales, and (c) to provide evidence about the differential validity of the scores. Using the CAS instrument (Loyd & Gressard, 1984), the authors measured the attitudes of 114 K-12 teachers. Loyd and Loyd examined the data from the four subscales of the CAS instrument: (a) computer anxiety, (b) computer confidence, (c) computer liking, and (d) computer usefulness. Their findings included a correlation between the subscales of anxiety and confidence (0.83). According to Loyd and Loyd, all four subscales were "related closely enough to support the use of the Total Score as a measure of general anxiety" (p. 908). The results obtained from use of this instrument further supported the validity of the CAS instrument and expanded its applicability to a different population.

Replicating the study done by Loyd and Loyd (1985), Koohang (1987) also set out to benchmark preservice teachers' attitudes toward computer technology. Using the CAS instrument (Loyd & Gressard, 1984), he focused on three independent variables and their potential impact on computer attitudes: gender, the amount of prior experience with computers, and the nature of that experience. The 60 college students selected as the subjects of this study were all preservice teachers, and results showed that there was a significant difference in overall computer experience and attitudes toward computers. Based upon these findings, Koohang (1989) recommended preservice teachers should be required to participate in a formal computer training course, which will lead to a higher positive attitude toward computers. The author then conducted further research in a 1989 study, attempting to answer the research question, "is there a difference between the levels of each independent variable considered separately and the four computer attitude scales of the Computer Attitude Scale instrument?" (pp. 140-141). Koohang (1989) again used the CAS instrument and collected additional variables, such as gender, keyboard familiarity, and word processing knowledge, to see if these variables correlated with attitudes toward computers. Eighty-one college students participated in the study, and Koohang (1989) discovered that there was no significant difference between gender and computer attitudes but computer experience did impact attitudes toward computers as did computer keyboarding experience, computer programming experience, and word processing experience.

Wanting to further explore this phenomenon of attitudes toward computers within the teacher population, Loyd and Gressard (1986) set out to analyze two specific variables and their potential impact on attitudes toward computers: gender and the amount of computer experience. Using the CAS (Loyd & Gressard, 1984), the authors of this study surveyed 112 teachers participating in a staff development program in Virginia, United States. In addition to the CAS, data were collected on gender and experience (defined as *none, less than 6 months, 6 months to 1 year,* and *more than 1 year*). Findings indicated that teachers with more than 1 year of experience with computers were less anxious than those with less experience, males were significantly less anxious than females, and males were significantly more confident with computers than females. Finally, those teachers with at least 6 months of experience with computers perceived computers to be more useful than those with less than 6 months of experience with computers. The authors concluded that their findings regarding gender and computer anxiety were contrary to other studies done (Loyd & Gressard, 1984), yet they attributed these differences to the selected population (teachers). Although the authors' overlying conclusion from these explorations of the CAS and its results concluded that experience is closely related to attitudes toward computers (Loyd & Gressard, 1984, 1986; Loyd & Loyd, 1985), the authors recommended further exploration on these findings.

Yet another effort to establish the reliability, factor validity and fit to a unidimensional model for the CAS (Loyd & Gressard, 1984) was made by Kluever, Lam, Hoffman, Green, and Swearingen (1994). The authors of this study distributed the revised

CAS (Loyd & Loyd, 1985) to 265 subjects participating in a teacher-development program to enhance their use of computer technology in the classroom setting. Using a pre- and posttest format, Kluever et al. received very similar results to the study done by Loyd and Loyd, with the reliability of the total scale for the posttest score of 0.94. Scores did change significantly between pre- and posttests with 32 of the 40 items significantly different at the 0.05 level. Overall, the data from this study suggest that the CAS is a reliable instrument in the measurement of teacher attitudes toward computers. The significant differences between pre- and posttest indicates a successful use of the intervention for the subjects (in this case a training program). However, the authors noted caution at the generalizability of this study, as the subjects (teachers who volunteered for the computer training program, generally having computer experience) could bias the results.

Validating multiple scales that measure attitudes toward computers. By the early 1990s, there appeared to be a myriad of computer attitude scales available to educators, but as Woodrow (1991) noted, "educators are faced with the problem of which one to choose" (p. 166). Woodrow (1991) wanted to compare empirically the reliability and factorial validity of four computer attitude scales using a single population sample; the intercorrelations among these scales; and their individual correlations with age, gender, computer experience, computer literacy, and computer achievement. Using the CAS (Loyd & Gressard, 1984), Computer Use Questionnaire (Griswold, 1983), Attitudes Toward Computers (Reece & Gable, 1982), and Computer Survey (Stevens, 1980), Woodward (1991) surveyed 98 students in her study, and the author found overall the four scales evaluated were "remarkably similar" (p. 181). Specifically, Woodrow (1991) found her results similar to those of Gressard and Loyd (1985) for the CAS, and specifically recommended this instrument for use with computer novices.

Like Woodrow (1991), other studies done by Gardner, Discenza, and Dukes (1993) and Moroz and Nash (1997b) attempted to examine the validity and reliability among multiple instruments. In Gardner et al.'s (1993) study, the authors empirically compared four measures of attitude toward computers with two goals in mind. First, they hoped to determine which of the instruments being examined was superior to the others regarding reliability and validity. Second, they hoped to identify a small number of items from the four instruments being examined in order to create a short, highly reliable instrument for measuring attitudes toward computers. Gardner et al. found that the four instruments--Attitudes Towards Computers (Raub, 1981), the CAS (Loyd & Gressard, 1984), the CAIN (Simonson et al., 1987), and the Blomberg-Lowery Computer Attitude Task (Erickson, 1987)--were "essentially equal in terms of reliability and validity" (p. 487) and suggested that using any one of these four scales would be "more than adequate measures of computer attitudes" (p. 493). Thus, the researcher did not conclude with the development of a shorter scale.

In Moroz and Nash's (1997b) study, the authors sought to examine the factorial structure of the two most researched instruments to date: the BCCAS developed by Bear et al. (1987) and its convergent validity with the popular four-scale version of the CAS (Loyd & Loyd, 1985). Although to this point the BCCAS has been analyzed numerous times to verify its validity and reliability (e.g., Bear et al.; Francis & Evans, 1995; Pike et al., 1993), Moroz and Nash (1997b) noted that none of these studies examined an American adult sample, thus questioning the generalizability of the BCCAS. In order to establish the BCCASs concurrent validity, the authors also administered the CAS (Loyd & Loyd) due to its history of validity and reliability on a variety of populations. Using a sample of 222 American graduate students and analyzing the results of the BCCAS as compared to the CAS, they concluded that the BCCAS was internally consistent and predicative of a range of attitudinal domains towards computers.

However, the most extensive study done around existing instruments measuring attitudes toward computers was recently conducted by Christensen and Knezek (2000). The authors of this study examined the internal consistency reliabilities of 14 existing instruments that purport to measure attitudes toward computers. Because many of these instruments had been developed more than a decade ago, the authors of this study set out to determine whether the scales, as originally published, were still reliable.

The following instruments were included in Christensen and Knezek's (2000) analysis: CAS (Gressard & Loyd, 1985), Computer Use Questionnaire (Griswold, 1983), Attitudes Toward Computers Scale (Reece & Gable, 1982), Computer Survey Scale (Stevens, 1980), CARS (Heissen et al., 1987), Attitudes Towards Computers (Raub, 1981), Blomberg-Lowery Computer Attitude Task (Erickson, 1987), Attitude Toward Computer Scale (Francis, 1993), CAM (Kay, 1993a), Computer Attitude Questionnaire (Knezek & Miyashita, 1994), Computer Attitude Items (Pelgrum, Janssen Reinen, & Plomp, 1993), Computer Attitudes Scale for Secondary Students (T. Jones & Clarke, 1994), and E-Mail (D'Souza, 1992). These instruments were used to create one larger, 284-question instrument, called the Teachers' Attitudes Toward Computers Questionnaire. It was implemented to 621 teachers in Texas, Florida, New York, and California. Their results yielded that most of the instruments that originally had higher internal consistency reliabilities (Chronbach's Alpha) remained close to the same levels. One noted exception was the Loyd and Gressard (1984) CSA instrument with an alpha that decreased from 0.86 when originally developed in 1986 to 0.75 in 1995. However,

Christensen and Knezek noted that this is still respectable and that "especially worthy are those subscales which exhibit high reliability without excessive length" (p. 329). With this large body of research establishing a variety of instruments' overall validity and reliability regarding the measure of attitudes toward computers, the field has several instruments from which to choose.

Section summary. To summarize, researchers eventually expanded their description of attitude beyond the limited definition of just anxiety. Stevens (1980, 1982), Raub (1981), Reece and Gable (1982), and Griswold (1983) all conducted research on college students, teachers, or both to measure the phenomena of computer anxiety, creating several different instruments. Bear et al. (1987) created the BCCAS, a widely used instrument to measure this phenomenon. Various researchers subsequently used this instrument on a variety of student populations worldwide, including American, South African, Indian, Welsh, and Israeli students (Francis & Evans, 1995; Katz et al., 1995; Miller & Varma, 1993; Pike et al., 1993; Yaghi, 1997). Unfortunately, to date, no exploration of the BCCAS and it applicability to nonacademic settings in the United States or any other country has been conducted.

Woodrow (1991) stated that the most widely used instrument regarding the measurement of the phenomena of attitudes toward computer is the CAS by Loyd and Gressard (1984). Studies repeatedly provided data to support the overall validity and reliability of the instrument on a variety of populations but mostly American college students and teachers (e.g., Kluever et al., 1994; Koohang, 1986, 1987; Loyd & Loyd, 1985; Pope-Davis & Twig, 1991). Several researchers attempted to analyze empirically various instruments purported to measure attitudes toward computers (e.g., Christensen & Knezek, 2000; Gardner et al., 1993; Moroz & Nash, 1997b; Woodrow, 1991). Although they concluded that all instruments analyzed did produce data to support each instruments' overall validity and reliability, many suggested (e.g., Gardner et al., 1993; Kluever et al., 1994; Woodrow, 1991) using Loyd and Gressard's (1984) CAS due to its longevity, length, and body of research, including those who compared the CAS with the BCCAS (Bear et al., 1987).

Researchers analyzed demographic variables and attitudes toward computers to see if any correlations existed. Pope-Davis and Twig (1991) found that age did significantly influence attitude toward computers and computer experience was a significant factor only on the liking subscale and not the other subscales as other studies have found. Overall, researchers found mixed outcomes with regard to gender and computer attitudes (e.g., Koohang, 1986; Loyd & Gressard, 1986; Pope-Davis & Twig, 1991), but overwhelming support was found for the correlation between prior computer experience and attitudes toward computers (e.g., Koohang, 1986, 1987, 1989; Loyd & Gressard, 1986; Loyd & Loyd, 1985; Woodrow, 1991). Appendix A summarizes the key findings from this area of the literature review; Appendix B provides further detail of the literature reviewed in this section in table format.

Measures for Computer Literacy, Competence, and Aptitude

As Simonson et al. (1987) noted, "prior to the mid-1970s, the term *computer literacy* was not often found in the literature" (p. 232). However, as computer technology became increasingly more prominent in the American education system, many researchers sought to measure the level of computer literacy concretely among students and faculty alike. In an early study on the need of computer literacy, Molnar (1978) noted that the United States possessed a national need to foster computer literacy. Further, if we are to meet this need,

we must ensure that high school graduates have an understanding of the uses and

applications of the computer in society and its effect upon their everyday lives.

. . . A nation concerned with its social needs and economic growth cannot be

indifferent to the problems of literacy. If we are to reap the benefits of science-

driven industries, we must develop a computer-literate society. (p. 36)

The National Center for Educational Statistics (1983) defined computer literacy as

"whatever a person needs to know and do with computers in order to function

competently in our information-based society" (p. 8). In addition, the term aptitude has

become synonymous with literacy, defining the characteristics of a person that forecasts

his or her probability of success under a given scenario" (Snow, 1976).

The Minnesota Educational Computing Consortium sponsored an early attempt to

develop a standard instrument to measure computer literacy for K-12 students, called the

Minnesota Computer Literacy and Awareness Assessment (MCLAA; spearheaded by

Anderson et al., 1980). The authors developed the instrument through the use of subject-

matter experts incorporating data from educational objectives, course descriptions,

curriculum guides, and evaluative instrument of actual compute courses. This helped

define computer literacy as being comprised of six dimensions: (a) hardware, (b)

software, (c) programming and algorithms, (d) applications, (e) social impact, and (f)

affect (subdivided into computer enjoyment, computer anxiety, and self-confidence in

computing). The authors developed the instrument around these six dimensions and

administered the instrument to high school students both entering and leaving computer

courses in a random sample from across the state of Minnesota in 1978. Results from the

study showed that females high school students performed better than their male counterparts in some specific areas of computer programming, such as algorithmic applications where problems are verbal versus mathematic. The author concluded that this finding, contrary to much of the data regarding male and female performance in mathematics, implies that the MCLAA is free from mathematic bias, and further supports it construct validity (Anderson, 1987). Anderson and Klassen (1981) then used the definition of computer literacy as defined for the MCLAA to develop instructional modules for K-12 students around these six dimensions. The authors noted that, even in the early 1980s, the "technological context and the educational environment [were] changing very rapidly" (Anderson & Klassen, p. 133) and thus wanted to readdress the instructional strategies for use with the MCLAA.

Bitter and Davis (1985) set out to gather updated data from two previous studies done to measure teacher attitudes toward computers and their computer literacy. Using the MCLAA (Anderson et al., 1980), the authors conducted a longitudinal study, surveying a total of 240 American teachers enrolled in a computer training course over a 2-year period. The instrument was in two facets: looking at the phenomena of attitude toward computers and computer knowledge. Regarding the dimension of attitude, Bitter and Davis found that, over the 2-year period, participants' overall attitudes toward computers remained fairly consistent with minor concerns around the increasing persuasiveness of computers in society. Regarding the dimension of knowledge, the MCLAA's overall weighted mean score was 42.33, or 79.8% of the total number of points possible, meaning overall the teachers were knowledgeable about computers as measured by the MCCLAA. However as Kay (1993b) noted of the instrument, the "cognitive component of the scale incorporated questions primarily based on technical areas related to programming, algorithms, and hardware" (p. 17). Bitter and Davis overall determined that their subjects had an increasingly positive reception for computers in the classroom and in society overall. The subjects expressed an interest in preparing themselves to be computer literate and to be able to teach others about computer literacy. The authors concluded that more in-service continuing education needed to be conducted in order to develop teachers to be prepared for teaching computer literacy to future students. Most importantly, Bitter and Davis determined that there was a positive correlation of $r = +0.72$ between average attitudes toward computers and the average level of computer knowledge the teachers possessed, meaning the higher the level of computer knowledge, the more positive the attitudes toward computers.

Although the MCLAA (Anderson et al., 1980) and other instruments sought to measure computer literacy, there was still much disparity between the definitions of this phenomenon. This ambiguity prompted Gabriel (1985) to develop a new instrument to look at this phenomenon. The author reported on the K-12 curriculum development on the concept of computer literacy implemented in the worldwide Department of Defense Dependents school system, which mimicked the concepts of the Minnesota Educational Computer Consortium as identified by Anderson et al. (1980). Gabriel defined computer literacy as being comprised of four subdomains: (a) interacting with computers, (b) functions and uses of computers, (c) general problem-solving skills, and (d) applications and impact on society. The author also noted that computer science was comprised of three subdomains: (a) writing software, (b) hardware operations, and (c) using computers for problem solving. Within each one of these seven subdomains were several specific instructional objectives (totaling 30 learning objects); these were then divided into three tiers of proficiency. To develop the paper-based instrument for measuring these phenomena, the author created a series of instruments that looked at varying mixes of the four subdomains of computer literacy for each of the three tiers identified. For example, Tier 1 (administered at Grade 4), the instrument looked more at problem solving and less at impact on society, while at Tier 3 (administered at Grade 11), the emphasis was on impact on society and very little focus on the problem-solving attributes of computers. The author pilot tested the instruments in the spring of 1982 on 150 subjects. Revisions to the instruments were made, and a second distribution of tests occurred in the spring of 1983. Overall, the instruments were distributed to students within the Department of Defense Dependents school system and two additional K-12 school populations within the United States, comprising a large total subject population of 10,000.

The average scores for the tests in all grade levels for Gabriel's (1985) study were around 50% correct. According to Gabriel, general problem-solving skills declined after the first tier (Grade 4), meaning that "students are less likely to acquire knowledge or skills related to this program objective outside of school than any of the others" (p. 158). Regarding the interest subdomain, over 80% of the students at each grade indicated they would like to learn much more about computers. A correlation was discovered between the increase of computer literacy and the amount of hands-on time the students receive on a computer. According to Gabriel, the data also suggested that, when comparing the results of the Department of Defense Dependents school system students to the two K-12 United States school samples, "essentially the same pattern [exists] across grade levels and subtests" (p. 161). The author stressed that the findings in this study should not be construed as representative of the entire United States K-12 population, but they are helpful in providing direction for further investigation.

As noted earlier in this review of the literature, Simonson et al. (1987) looked at defining computer literacy and computer anxiety in their study with a goal of creating a standardized test of computer literacy. The authors defined computer literacy as consisting of four subdomains: (a) computer attitudes, (b) computer applications, (c) computer systems, and (d) computer programming. They developed a list of 70 competencies for the computer literate person as dictated by a nationwide sample of instructional computing educators, and then they used this list to create an 80-question multiple-choice test. The authors distributed the instrument to 341 college students at six different universities, discovering a reliability of 0.86 for the instrument. Overall responders thought the instrument did measure computer literacy; the mean response to the question on the instrument, "Generally, does this definition meet with your concept of computer literacy?" was 3.94 ($SD = 0.81$) on a 5-point Likert scale.

Next to the MCLAA (Anderson et al., 1980), a second most widely used instrument developed to measure the phenomena of computer literacy was created by Murphy et al. (1988). The authors produced the Computer Self-Efficacy Scale (CSE) to measure perceptions of capability regarding specific computer-related knowledge and skills. After a review of the literature and an in-depth analysis of the skills emphasized in three different graduate courses designed to teach micro and mainframe computer-related skills, the authors of this study developed the 32 question 5-point Likert scale instrument. A participant's high score on the CSE indicates a high degree of confidence in one's computer abilities.

Murphy et al. (1988) distributed their instrument to 414 graduate students and nurses. Their factor analysis yielded a three-factor solution based upon the skill level it would take to accomplish the computer-related tasks of each of the 32 items on the instrument. These levels included beginning-level computer skills (16 items), advanced-level computer skills (13 items), and mainframe computer skills (3 items). The coefficient alpha levels for the three factors were 0.97, 0.96, and 0.93, respectively. The authors

concluded that the data suggest males and females have varying degrees of self-reported

computer skills.

An additional study by Karsten and Roth (1998) looked at the work of Murphy et

al. (1988), but it explored the relationships among computer experience, computer self-

efficacy, and computer-dependent performance in an introductory computer literacy

course. Using CSE (Murphy et al.), Karsten and Roth assessed college students'

computer experience and computer self-efficacy prior to participation in the course and

analyzed their relationship to subsequent course performance. Their results suggest that it

is the relevance of computer experience students bring to the classroom that is most

predictive of performance, not the amount of computer experience or exposure. In

addition, they found only computer self-efficacy to be significantly related to computer-

dependent course performance.

Even though the CSE (Murphy et al., 1988) continued to be widely used in a

number of studies (Gardner et al., 1993; Harrison & Rainer, 1992, 1996; Karsten & Roth,

1998; Murphy et al.), conflicting results in its validity and reliability prompted Moroz

and Nash (1997a) to refine the CSE instrument originally created by Murphy et al. Based

upon the data collected, the authors' results concluded that the scale also distinguishes

between users with high and low amounts of computer use experience. They also

concluded that the CSE is measuring the same construct to a similar degree for high and

low computer users. The results of this research show that the CSE scale is suitable for

use in research and evaluation if the construct under inspection is that of computer self-

efficacy. It must be noted, however, that the domains are specific and any attempt to

generalize results across other computer-related knowledge and skill areas was not recommended.

Although research continued on the development of measures for computer literacy, the debate over the definition remained. Kay (1993b) noted that the definitions of computer literacy to date were either too narrow or too broad and thus did not allow for the opportunity to analyze comparative results effectively. In addition, Kay (1993b) noted that most existing instruments "are dated and lean heavily on technological and programming content" (p. 17); thus, the existing instruments' area of measurement may be obsolete with the development of technology and the ease of computer usage. Kay (1993b) stated, "with the widespread introduction of the microcomputer and user-friendly application software, it has become increasingly easy to use computers, often requiring only the ability to read and write to perform highly sophisticated maneuvers" (p. 17).

Because of this, Kay (1993b) developed a new instrument, the Computer Ability Survey, to measure four subscales of computer literacy: (a) software ability, (b) computer awareness, (c) programming skills, and (d) perceived control. Included was a section for demographic data collection. The instrument used a 7-point Likert scale. The author's sample consisted of 647 preservice teachers from four universities across Ontario, Canada. Kay (1993b) found that, although subjects had a low knowledge of software ($M = 33.52$; $SD = 13.5$ with a possible range of 10–70), they had an even lower knowledge of computer programming ($M = 10.1$; $SD = 6.5$ with the possible range of 5–35). Regarding perceived control, subjects perceived that they had more control over what they wanted the computer to do ($M = 4.2$) and were less likely to say they needed an experienced person near them ($M = 3.6$). Overall, correlations between the Computer Ability Survey subscales were high and significant ($p < 0.001$). The author discovered significant positive correlations among all the computer ability subscales and mathematical ability, attitudes toward computers, and an independent measure of software ability as noted in the CAM instrument (Kay, 1993a). Kay (1993b) noted that there does exist potential bias in these results as the subjects were predominantly female, preservice teachers from a rural area. However, Kay (1993b) stated that the findings do suggest that the Computer Ability Survey is a "practical, multicomponent, easy-to-administer research tool for assessing ability to use computers incorporating software ability, awareness, programming ability and perceived control subscales" (p. 25).

Despite this increasing body of research looking at the validity and reliability and use of various instruments purporting to measure computer attitudes, M. Jones and Pearson (1996) argued that, while many studies have investigated the phenomenon of computer literacy, "few studies have addressed the properties of the instruments used to measure this construct" (pp. 17-18). They argued that instruments to date are too subjective and rely heavily on the respondents' view of themselves to rate their level of computer knowledge. Therefore, M. Jones and Pearson attempted to develop an instrument to objectively measure this construct. Using cross-sectional and longitudinal data, M. Jones and Pearson administered a 12-question objective instrument around the participants' knowledge of computers. In addition, they administered a 26-item subjective instrument capturing the responders' perceptions of their computer skills. The data from this objective survey were gathered from 141 undergraduates in 1994 and were compared to data previously collected three times in other studies in 1989 ($N = 289$, $N = 295$) and 1990 ($N = 295$).

M. Jones and Pearson (1996) also tested a slightly modified version of the instrument, most notably omitting the option of "I don't know" in the response structure. Results indicated that the 1994 data collection completed by the authors was consistent with previous data collection; the mean score on the 1994 subjective test was 38 (out of a high score of 60). However, this low number worried the researchers: Why was there a low computer competence with the 1994 group (and the previous other groups)? Using comparative analysis, the researchers ruled out other possibilities to low scores (e.g., responders not taking the instrument seriously or the questions being too difficult), helping to establish the instrument's reliability. To establish the instrument's convergent validity, the authors looked at the correlation between computer literacy scores on the two instruments (both subjective and objective). They established that there was a strong correlation between the two instruments ($r = 0.49$, $p \leq 0.0001$ for basic computer skills section, and $r = 0.36$, $p \leq 0.0001$ for advanced computer skills section), while the modified instrument did not retain convergent validity. In conclusion, M. Jones and Pearson determined that it is important to retain the "I don't know" option in the instrument as this improves the instrument's validity and reliability.

One of the criticisms some authors noted in the measurements of computer literacy revolves around the concept of experience related to literacy, especially as computers expand into so many facets of the 21st-century modern lifestyle. Potosky and Bobko (1998) looked at previous studies around the occurrence of computer experience and developed the Computer Understanding and Experience Scale (CUES). They argued that many studies looked at frequency of computer use to determine experience, but computer understanding does not necessarily correlate to the frequency of computer usage. Therefore, they developed a new instrument around this phenomenon and attempted to determine the validity and reliability of this instrument through a quantitative study of 279 volunteers (mostly college students with a few full-time computer programming professionals). The CUES instrument was presented in a 5-point

Likert Scale format, and it provided the authors with much data to conduct such statistical analysis as factor analysis done based upon the Kaiser-Guttman rule, multiple *t* tests for construct validity, and correlational analysis. They concluded that their CUES is a convenient, internally consistent measure that rates participants' self-perceived level of computer competence. The authors noted that a high score on the CUES reflected a person's high self-perception of their computer knowledge.

To summarize, the National Center for Education Statistics (1983) defined computer literacy as "whatever a person needs to know and do with computers in order to function competently in our information-based society" (p. 8). The Minnesota Educational Computing Consortium sponsored an early attempt to develop a standard instrument to measure computer literacy for K-12 students called the MCLAA (Anderson et al., 1980). Using their six dimensions of computer literacy, the authors developed the instrument and administered it to high school students across the state of Minnesota in 1978. Results showed that female students performed better than their male counterparts in some specific areas of computer programming where problems are verbal versus mathematic. Bitter and Davis (1985) also used the MCLAA. Their study concluded that, over the 2-year period, participants' overall attitudes toward computers remained fairly consistent and a positive correlation between average attitudes toward computers and the average level of computer knowledge existed among their subjects.

Murphy et al.'s (1988) CSE was one of the more popular instruments measuring this phenomena (e.g., Gardner et al., 1993; Harrison & Rainer, 1992, 1996; Karsten and Roth, 1998; Murphy et al.). Data from the initial pilot study of the instrument suggested the instrument was valid and reliable, and males and females have varying degrees of self-reported computer skills. Subsequent studies done with the CSE (e.g., Gardner et al.,

1993; Harrison & Rainer, 1992, 1996; Karsten & Roth, 1998; Moroz & Nash, 1997a) suggested that it is the relevance of computer experience students bring to the classroom that is most predictive of performance, not the amount of computer experience or exposure. In addition, Karsten and Roth (1998) found only computer self-efficacy to be significantly related to computer-dependent course performance. Even when Moroz and Nash (1997a) refined the CSE (Murphy et al., 1988), they came to similar conclusions as the instrument's developers.

A reoccurring trend with regard to the measurement of self-reported computer competence was that, as technology changed, so too did the definition of what researchers determined to be important aspects of computer literacy. Researchers such as Gabriel (1985) developed a new instrument to look at this phenomena. Subjects reported average scores of around 50% correct, and a correlation was discovered between the increase of computer literacy and the amount of hands-on time the students receive on a computer. Similarly, Simonson et al. (1987) also developed an instrument to measure computer literacy, which was based upon a different definition of what the term computer literacy means. Their initial pilot study determined it to be a valid and reliable measure for the phenomena. Kay (1993b) developed the CAS to measure the author's definition of computer literacy, and positive correlations were discovered between all the computer ability subscales and mathematical ability, attitudes toward computers, and an independent measure of software ability. M. Jones and Pearson (1996) also developed an instrument to measure this phenomena and found overall low computer competence scores for their subjects. The authors of this study determined that it is important to retain the "I don't know" option in the instrument as this improves the instrument's validity and reliability. Using a more contemporary definition of computer literacy, Potosky and

Bobko (1998) developed the CUES, and the data from their pilot supported the overall validity and reliability of this instrument. Appendix C summarizes the key findings from this area of the literature review; Appendix D provides further detail of the literature reviewed in this section in table format.

Measures of Both Attitude Toward Computers and Computer Literacy

Interestingly, many researchers initially examined the phenomena of attitudes toward computers and computer literacy separately, but some early researchers hypothesized that computer experience is significantly related to computer anxiety (Koohang, 1986; Loyd & Gressard, 1984; Simonson et al., 1987) and sought to measure the correlation between these constructs. This, in turn, led to a plethora of studies and instruments purported to examine both phenomena simultaneously.

In a National Science Foundation-funded research project, Roszkowski, Devlin, Snelbecker, Aiken, and Jacobsohn (1988) set out to examine computer aptitude, literacy, interest, and overall attitudes toward computers. At the time of the study, no succinct instrument was available that looked at all of the above-mention phenomena, so researchers used two instruments to look at the phenomena. Their research reported on the stability of two instruments over the National Science Foundation training of educators and the validity and reliability of the two instruments and their interrelationship.

The 42 subjects who participated in Roszkowski et al.'s (1988) examination were teachers from a variety of backgrounds undergoing a training program sponsored by the National Science Foundation to be retrained in computer science. The authors of this study used the Computer Aptitude, Literacy, and Interest Profile (CALIP) by Poplin, Drew, and Gable (1984), an instrument that purported to measure computer aptitude, literacy, and interest. Even though interest is a construct of attitude, Roszkowski et al. wanted to explore attitude further and thus also administered the CAS by Loyd and Gressard (1984). Using a test-retest method, subjects were given both CALIP and CAS at the beginning of the program and then 11 months later at the end of the program. It was concluded that the instruments were stable over the time period. Overall, the authors deduced that the CAS was shown to exhibit comparable validity to the CALIP. They noted that the prospective usefulness of the (at the time) still-in development CAS "is surprising, given the typically poor reliability and validity of many, if not most, measures of attitudes" (p. 1034).

Woodrow (1992) conducted a pretest-posttest study to measure preservice teacher computer literacy and attitudes toward computers, using several instruments to look at these two phenomena. Woodrow utilized the MCLAA (Anderson et al., 1980) to analyze the phenomena of computer literacy, and the author used four different scales to measure the phenomenon of computer attitudes: (a) the CAS (Loyd & Gressard, 1984), (b) Attitude Toward Computers (Reece & Gable, 1982), (c) the Computer Survey instrument (Stevens, 1980, 1982), and (d) the Computer-Ability Gender Equality developed by Woodrow (1992). The amalgamated instrument measured three aspects of computer literacy (usage, operations, and applications) and six dimensions of attitude (anxiety, confidence, liking, interest, awareness, and gender ability). With this instrument, the author set out to accomplish the following: (a) determine if a programming-focused computer training course provided significant improvements in students' attitudes toward computers or their level of computer competence, (b) determine if there are demographic variables that affect computer attitudes or computer literacy, and (c) determine if there are improvements in a students' attitude toward computers or level of computer literacy correlated with success in a programming-oriented computer training course.

Woodrow (1992) administered the above-named instruments to a sample of 36 preservice teachers enrolled in a computer training course of which approximately 80% of the curriculum involved learning to program in the BASIC computer language. With the exception of the attitude dimension of computer confidence and literacy dimension of computer usage, all dimensions of attitude and computer literacy increased significantly between the pretest and posttest of the subjects. Interestingly, subjects' attitude gains were significantly correlated with achievement in the course with the exception of the gender-ability dimension. Woodrow (1992) noted, however, that correlations to computer literacy and success in the computer training course were only significant in one facet of the instrument: Computer Literacy Index (Anderson et al., 1980). Woodrow (1992) explained a potential reason for this variance is that the instrument used was not as applicable as it could have been given contemporary placement of computers in society and their use:

> The instrument used to measure computer literacy was selected on the basis of its status of a standard or frequency used measure of computer literacy. However, the MCLAA instrument was developed before the advent of wide-spread availability and use of microcomputers and contains references to terms more relevant to mainframe computers than to microcomputers. (p. 214)

Woodrow (1992) also noted that there were no significant changes in either relationship to gender in entry-level computer attitudes or toward the attitudes of computers at the end of the intervention. The author hypothesized that the instructional approach to hands-on activities coupled with the emphasis on education-related software programs attributed to this phenomena remaining consistent among the genders.

Although the findings of this study indicated that the creation and implementation of a training program around basic computer programming (a dimension of computer literacy) for preservice teachers would produce improvement in their general attitudes toward computers, Woodrow (1992) asked, "is programming really a necessary skill or is it just a hurdle to the acquisition of the skills that the students really want and will actually use?" (p. 217). Woodrow suggested that further investigation into this interesting question around computer attitude and computer literacy.

Expanding on her previous research (Woodrow, 1992), Woodrow (1994) then studied the implementation of several instruments that measured computer–related attitudes. The author used four instruments in her investigation: (a) CAS (Loyd & Gressard, 1984), (b) Attitudes Toward Computers (Reece & Gable, 1982), (c) the MCLAA (Anderson et al., 1980), and (d) the Computer Survey (Koohang, 1987). Woodrow (1994) set out to answer these research questions: (a) What are the computer-related attitudes of students as they enter secondary education? (b) What student attributes are correlated with these attitudes? (c) How stable are secondary students' computer-related attitudes? and (d) Does computer training produce significant gains in secondary students' computer-related attitudes? Interestingly, she found the greatest variance in attitudes toward computers occurred through unstructured computer experience and word processing experience, while gains in computer attitudes were independent of gender, computer training experience, and computer course achievement.

Harrison and Rainer (1992) argued that, although there are many reported measures of attitudes towards computers and aptitude of computers, they set out to examine the psychometric properties of three specific scales: two focused on computer attitudes. The scales were the CAS by Loyd and Gressard (1984) and the CARS by

Heissen et al. (1987). One scale focused on computer aptitude: the CSE by Murphy et al. (1988). Notably, the study's subjects consisted of 776 adults, all employees of a large American university but from a wide variety of areas within the university environment. They found that high anxiety (as reported in the CARS instrument) correlated with negative feelings toward computers (as reported in the CAS) and lower self-reported computer skill level (as reported in the CSE). Conversely, higher confidence (as reported in the CARS) correlated with positive attitudes (as reported in the CAS) and higher self-reported computer skills (as reported in the CSE). In conclusion, the authors of this particular study found the results encouraging that these three instruments do measure the phenomena in question and support their overall concurrent validity.

Delcourt and Kinzie (1993) noted that previous studies focused on distinct populations--children (Bear et al., 1987; Loyd & Gressard, 1984) and college students (Francis, 1993; Kay, 1993a)--and argued that little exists that is specifically targeted toward teacher education students and practicing teachers. Delcourt and Kinzie focused their energies on the development of two complimentary instruments around attitudes toward computers and computer aptitude: the Attitudes Toward Computer Technologies (ACT) instrument and the Self-Efficacy with Computer Technologies (SCT) instrument. The ACT instrument examined perceived usefulness of and the level of anxiety with computer technologies, and the SCT looks at perceived self-efficacy with certain computer technologies (word processing, e-mail usage, and CD-ROM database familiarity). For the ACT, the authors used modified items from existing instruments (Delcourt & Lewis, 1987; Loyd & Gressard, 1984; Murphy et al., 1988) in addition to items developed by the authors in conjunction with subject-matter experts. Delcourt and Kinzie developed the SCT items with assistance from subject-matter experts in computer technology education. The authors administered the 19-item ACT and the 25-item SCT instruments to 328 undergraduate and graduate students at six American universities. Internal consistency reliability estimates of 0.89 for the ACT and a 0.97 for the SCT were achieved. Overall, Delcourt and Kinzie found that attitudes were statistically significant predictors of self-efficacy for all three types of computer technologies (word processing, e-mail, and CD-ROM database usage). It is important to note that the Self-Efficacy with Computer Technologies (SCT) instrument was one of the first instruments to look at electronic mail as a standard application of comfort for computer technology.

Expanding the use of the ACT and SCT (Delcourt & Kinzie, 1993), Milbrath and Kinzie (2000) examined the changes in perceived anxiety with and usefulness of computer technology, frequency of using various computer functions (word processing, e-mail, spreadsheets, etc.), and perceived self-efficacy on six areas of computer usage in a longitudinal study on preservice teachers. Using the Computer Technology Survey, an amalgamated instrument combining the ACT and the SCT (Delcourt & Kinzie), Milbrath and Kinzie looked at two groups of prospective teachers over a 4-year period with multiple interventions throughout their tenure. The data revealed that, between the first instrument implementation and the middle of the longitudinal study, participants did not have a significant change in their perception of computer usefulness or comfort with computers. However, between this intervention and the final instrument dissemination, participants' comfort with computers and frequency of word processing usage increased significantly. Milbrath and Kinzie concluded that more frequent use of various facets of computers (word processing, spreadsheet usage, etc.) would yield high self-efficacy and comfort with that particular facet of computer technology.

Smith and Necessary (1996) set out to replicate the two studies done by Kay

(1993a, 1993b) around the phenomena of computer attitudes and self-reported computer literacy among college students. Specifically, the purpose of their study was to look at subjects' computer literacy levels and their attitudes toward computers based upon specific demographic areas (gender, age, and experience with computers). Using the CAS and the CAM (Kay, 1993a, 1993b), Smith and Necessary implemented the instrument to 316 college students, 83% of which were traditional college aged while the remainder were classified as nontraditional students (age > 23). Computer experience varied with the majority of the subjects having 4 or more years of experience ($N = 170$). Overall, Smith and Necessary had similar findings to Kay's studies (1993a, 1993b). They found that males scored significantly higher in their attitudes toward computers than females ($M = 90.6$ for males, $M = 81.8$ for females). In addition, statistically significant findings occurred with the years of computer use and higher self-reported computer ability and more frequent weekly use of a computer and higher self-reported computer aptitude. Smith and Necessary noted, however, that, in their ANOVA analysis of gender and its interaction to computer experience, these data could suggest "females score lower on computer literacy than their male counterparts because they have less computer-related experience, yet their scores may increase markedly as they are [sic] gain training" (p. 193). Therefore, the authors noted that, when analyzing demographic variables in relationship to computer literacy, one must take into account that a variable does not cause the level of computer literacy, but these variables exist together, and deeper efforts should be made to understand all the variables that could contribute to the differences in computer literacy among subjects.

To summarize, many researchers initially examined the phenomena of attitudes toward computers and computer literacy separately, but some early researchers hypothesized that computer experience is significantly related to computer anxiety (Koohang, 1986; Loyd & Gressard, 1984; Simonson et al., 1987) and sought to measure the correlation between these constructs. This, in turn, led to a plethora of studies and instruments purported to examine both phenomena simultaneously. Roszkowski et al. (1988) used the CALIP by Poplin et al. (1984) and the CAS by Loyd and Gressard (1984) to explore the two phenomena. The authors deduced that the CAS was shown to exhibit comparable validity to the CALIP. Woodrow (1992) used several existing instruments to examine these two phenomena, including the Computer-Ability Gender Equality developed by the author. Data suggested that, with the exception of attitude dimension of computer confidence and literacy dimension of computer usage, all dimensions of attitude and computer literacy increased significantly between the pretest and posttest of the subjects. Interestingly, subjects' attitude gains were significantly correlated with achievement in the course with the exception of the gender-ability dimension.

Woodrow (1992) noted, however, that correlations to computer literacy and success in the computer training course were only significant in one facet of the instrument: Computer Literacy Index (Anderson et al., 1980). The author also questioned the finding that, although the intervention of a basic computer programming class did improve subjects' general attitudes toward computers, Woodrow (1992) asked, "is programming really a necessary skill or is it just a hurdle to the acquisition of the skills that the students really want and will actually use?" (p. 217). Woodrow (1994) further explored the phenomena using four existing instruments that purported to measure the two phenomena, but in this study, they found the greatest variance in attitudes toward computers occurred through unstructured computer experience and word processing experience. Gains in computer attitudes were independent of gender, computer training experience, and computer course achievement.

Three studies used existing instruments to look at the phenomena of attitudes toward computers and self-reported computer competence. Harrison and Rainer (1992) found that high anxiety correlated with negative feelings toward computers and lower self-reported computer skill level. Conversely, they also found higher confidence correlated with positive attitudes (and higher self-reported computer skills). Delcourt and Kinzie (1993) discovered that attitudes were statistically significant predictors of self-efficacy for all three types of computer technologies (word processing, e-mail, and CD-ROM database usage). Milbrath and Kinzie (2000) determined that, between the first instrument implementation and the middle of the longitudinal study, participants did not have a significant change in their perception of computer usefulness or comfort with computers. They concluded that more frequent use of various facets of computers (word processing, spreadsheet usage, etc.) would yield high self-efficacy and comfort with that particular facet of computer technology. Finally, Smith and Necessary (1996) set out to replicate the two studies done by Kay (1993a, 1993b) and had similar findings to the original studies: (a) males scored significantly higher in their attitude toward computers than females and (b) statistically significant correlations between the years of computer use and higher self-reported computer ability and more frequent weekly use of a computer and higher self-reported computer aptitude. Appendix E summarizes the key findings from this area of the literature review; Appendix F provides further detail of the literature reviewed in this section in table format.

Measures of Attitude Toward End-User Software and Multimedia Instruction or e-Learning

Most studies done to date around attitudes toward computers and computer literacy referred to the overall machine itself; with few exceptions (Delcourt & Kinzie, 1993; Levine & Donitsa-Schmidt, 1997) did researchers incorporate any particular computer applications into their instruments. In today's technological learning environment, it takes more than a knowledge of computers to use e-learning effectively as a mechanism of instructional delivery; there needs to be an acceptable end-user satisfaction, which is sometimes referred to a Kirkpatrick 1 Level of Evaluation (Kirkpatrick, 1994) in order for learners to embrace their next foray into this type of medium (Rosenberg, 2001).

For this examination, e-learning (also referred to as technology-enabled learning) was defined as the use of such electronic media as CD-ROM, the Internet, private intranet, or any combination of these in order to facilitate training and education (Commission on Technology and Adult Learning, 2000; Urban & Weggen, 2000). Although these facets of this definition are technically types of media, each one is just a delivery mechanism for the instruction (Clark, 2001), and it is the content (as interfaced between the delivery medium and the student) that is instructional. E-learning is not the same as simple as posting a training workbook or course syllabus on a Web page, but it includes some method of interactivity for the learners (Sanders & Morrison-Shetlar, 2001).

Little investigation has occurred regarding the development and measurement of attitudes toward multimedia instruction (or e-learning). An early attempt to look at end-user attitudes toward computer satisfaction was done by Doll and Torkzadeh (1988). In their study, the authors created an instrument to measure end-user satisfaction for users who specifically interface with an application. It is important to understand that, at the time of this study, the current end-user and computer interaction through a graphic user interface application was fairly new; many computer users worked more closely with a person (an analyst or programmer) to accomplish tasks, write reports, or gather data from a database than performing these functions on their own through the use of software applications. However, Doll and Torkzadeh realized that "satisfaction leads to usage rather than usage stimulating satisfaction" (p. 260). Thus, their work is as applicable today looking at the satisfaction of an end user of a Web-based or computer-based training course as it was for their targeted applications in 1988.

Doll and Torkzadeh (1988) developed an instrument that measured five components of end-user satisfaction: (a) content, (b) accuracy, (c) format, (d) ease of use, and (d) timeliness. They first created a pool of 40 Likert-scale questions around these components and disseminated the instrument to 96 users in five corporate settings; these data were compared to a structured interview that captured the qualitative data from subjects. The authors determined which of the questions did not accurately measure the phenomenon in question through criterion-related validity tactics. This narrowed the instrument to 12 items and was redistributed to 618 end users, finding a reliability of 0.92 and criterion-related validity of 0.76. Doll and Torkzadeh noted that the successful use of this instrument "may be utilized to evaluate end-user applications" (p. 270). It was proven to be valid and reliable, and it could be used to benchmark end-users' attitudes toward computer applications.

Harrison and Rainer (1996) conducted a study to measure end-user satisfaction, hoping to establish the reliability and validity of an instrument that can be used to measure end-user satisfaction across a heterogeneous population. Further exploring the benefits of the End-User Computing Satisfaction Instrument created by Doll and Torkzadeh (1988), Harrison and Rainer (1996) set out to measure the validity and reliability of the instrument on 776 adults subjects, all employees of a large American university but from a wide variety of areas within the university environment. This population differed from the original done by Doll and Torkzadeh (1988), who focused on more "sophisticated" computer users than the 776 Harrison and Rainer (1996) used. The scale had four constructs (content, accuracy, ease of use, and timeliness), and reliability measures of 0.89, 0.65, 0.89, and 0.66, respectively, were observed by the authors; therefore, the instrument was concluded to be reliable (Harrison & Rainer, 1996). Based upon existing research (Harrison & Rainer, 1992), Harrison and Rainer (1996) also classified their end users into five categories of computer experience: (a) beginning end users, (b) intermediate end users, (c) advanced end users, (d) end-user facilitators, and (e) end-user infrastructure personnel. Perceptions of computer literacy were based upon subjects' responses to the CSE (Murphy et al., 1988). Based upon the findings of the data, Harrison and Rainer (1996) concluded that the EUCSI may be used "across all organizational personnel who used computers in their work and across all applications they employ" (p. 90). Like the research originally done by Doll and Torkzadeh, implications of Harrison and Rainer's (1996) research reached into the realm as to whether end users were satisfied with computer applications used for learning and teaching.

Spooner, Jordan, Algozzine, and Spooner (1999) sought to compare students' satisfaction and attitude toward two different instructional strategies–one incorporating electronic delivery and the other traditional face-to-face instruction–in a college education course. Although the authors acknowledged that the research on comparable studies yielded no significant difference between instructional delivery strategy (electronic versus traditional), other factors, such as student satisfaction, convenience, and interaction between students, yielded mixed results in a distance education delivery scenario. To examine this phenomenon, the authors used the existing course evaluation with slight modifications to reflect the specific instructional delivery method used. Internal consistency estimates were obtained for the total evaluation instrument, yielding a 0.98 reliability. Analyzing the results from the 51 college student (15 face-to-face and 36 via distance), Spooner et al. discovered no significant difference in overall satisfaction between the two course delivery methods, and students' opinions about the teaching skills of the instructor were not different between medium deliveries.

In one of the only studies to look at the three phenomena being addressed by this study, Koroghlanian and Brinkerhoff (2000) set out to assess the current state of college students' computer skills, their attitudes toward Internet-delivered instruction, and identify those components of an Internet course deemed important based on college students' demographics, computer experience, computer skills, and prior Internet-delivered course experience. The authors developed a five-section unnamed survey to collect the following data: (a) demographic information and amount of computer experience, (b) computer skills related to Internet-delivered courses, (c) attitudes toward and perceptions of Internet-delivered courses, (d) rating of components in Internet-delivered courses, and (e) prior Internet-delivered course experience. Koroghlanian and Brinkerhoff found that overall students' computer skills were relatively shallow, consisting of basic software skills. In addition, college students were generally neutral toward Internet-based instruction, with those having prior Internet instruction experience far less optimistic concerning the degree to which technology may interfere with learning. However, those with prior experience were more likely to recommend taking an Internet-delivered course.

67

Coll Garcia (2001) understood that many instruments had been created that focused on attitudes toward computers overall, but as Koroghlanian and Brinkerhoff (2000) noted, few focused specifically on learners' attitudes toward multimedia instruction. Coll Garcia created the Multimedia Attitude Survey, a 25-item instrument that looked at eight subscales of attitude toward multimedia. These included (a) students' attitudes toward computer interaction, (b) attitudes toward learner's control over the instructional process, (c) degree of involvement in the multimedia activity, (d) students' views on individualized instruction, (e) perceptions toward self-paced instruction, (f) attitudes toward the software used in terms of its user-friendliness, (g) students' level of anxiety when working with multimedia, and (h) general opinion towards the instructional application used. The author did not distinguish which of the 32 items in the instrument were newly created or used from existing surveys, but the author implemented the instrument to 40 Spanish college students in the initial pilot study. Findings resulted in the removal of 7 of the items due to lack of consistency with the other items in the instrument. The revised instrument proved to be a valid and reliable measure of the eight constructs of multimedia instruction, and they can be used individually or together. The author noted that, although the study showed the Multimedia Attitude Survey to be a reliable, valid instrument, the sample group used was relatively small ($N = 40$) and thus further testing should commence on the applicability of the instrument and the findings in this study.

Like Coll Garcia (2001), Sanders and Morrison-Shetlar (2001) wanted to understand the impact of a Web-based, instructional component within an American college environment and developed an instrument to measure students' attitudes toward Web-based instruction. Following an extensive literature review and content validity review, the authors developed the Web-Based Instruction Attitude Scale (Sanders & Morrison-Shetlar), which is a 19-item Likert-scale instrument with a reliability coefficient found to be 0.78. Although the subject's population was relatively small ($N = 110$), the authors found that the Web-based component added to the existing biology curriculum had a highly positive effect on student learning and overall attitudes toward the course. Interestingly, the authors found that females were significantly more positive toward the use of the Web-based instructional component than males, and females used the medium more frequently than males as well. Conversely, no significant correlation was found between ethnicity, year in school, age, or computer experience and attitudes toward the Web-based instructional component. The authors concluded that instructors should attempt to incorporate a Web-based component in instructional courses.

To summarize, few studies existed on the development and measurement of attitudes toward multimedia instruction (or e-learning). Doll and Torkzadeh (1988) made an early attempt to look at end-user attitudes toward computer satisfaction and developed an instrument to measure this construct. Their pilot study provided data to support the instrument's overall validity and reliability, and the authors suggested using the instrument to benchmark end-users' attitudes toward computer applications. Harrison and Rainer (1996) conducted similar research but on a different demographic population than Doll and Torkzadeh. Using the same instrument as Doll and Torkzadeh, Harrison and Rainer's (1996) study provided data to further support the validity and reliability of the instrument. Both studies reached into the realm as to whether end users were satisfied with computer applications used for learning and teaching. Spooner et al. (1999) sought to compare students' satisfaction and attitudes toward two different instructional strategies—one incorporating electronic delivery and the other traditional face-to-face instruction–in a college education course. The authors of this study discovered no significant difference in overall satisfaction between the two course delivery methods, and students' opinions about the teaching skills of the instructor were not different between medium deliveries.

Koroghlanian and Brinkerhoff (2000) conducted one of the only studies to look at the three phenomena being addressed by this author. After developing and implementing an instrument to measure the three phenomena (self-reported computer skills, attitudes toward Internet-delivered instruction, and attitudes toward computers), the authors not only found data to support the instrument's overall validity and reliability, but they also discovered overall subjects' computer skills were relatively shallow, consisting of basic software skills. They also found that subjects were generally neutral toward Internet-based instruction with those having prior Internet instruction experience far less optimistic concerning the degree to which technology may interfere with learning. Coll Garcia (2001) created an instrument to measure students' perceptions of multimedia instruction. The author of this study found that, although the data suggested the instrument is a reliable, valid instrument, the sample group used was relatively small and thus further testing should commence on the applicability of the instrument and the findings in this study.

Finally, Sanders and Morrison-Shetlar (2001) sought to measure the impact of a Web-based, instructional component within an American college environment. The authors developed an instrument to measure this phenomenon and found that the Web-based component added to the existing curriculum had a highly positive effect on student learning and overall attitudes toward the course. Interestingly, the authors found that females were significantly more positive toward the use of the Web-based instructional component than males and females used the medium more frequently than males as well. Conversely, no significant correlation was found between ethnicity, year in school, age, or computer experience and attitudes toward the Web-based instructional component. The author concluded that instructors should attempt to incorporate a Web-based component in instructional courses. Appendix G summarizes the key findings from this area of the literature review; Appendix H provides further detail of the literature reviewed in this section in table format.

Elements, Hypotheses, and Theories to Be Investigated

As identified in the literature, two factors could potentially impede the affect of computer-assisted learning before the adult learner even begins the learning session: (a) their individual competence with computers and (b) their attitude toward the technology itself. Therefore, the research study set out to develop, validate, and show the reliability of an instrument to measure subjects' attitudes toward computers, attitudes toward e-learning, and self-report computer aptitude. Because of various findings in the literature, the author also investigated the following six hypotheses in the proposed research study, using data garnered from pilot subjects:

1. Subjects' attitudes toward computers will be positively correlated with their attitude toward e-learning as a method of learning.

2. Subjects' age will be negatively correlated with self-reported computer competence.

3. Subjects' age will be negatively correlated with attitudes toward e-learning.

4. Subjects' level of education will be positively correlated with their attitudes toward e-learning.

5. Subjects' self-reported computer competence will be positively correlated with

overall attitudes toward e-learning.

      6. There will be no significant difference between gender and attitudes toward computers, attitudes toward technology-enabled learning, and self-reported computer competence.

Summary of the Phenomena and Contribution This Study Will Make to the Field

      Given this review of the literature, several trends emerged as well as several areas of opportunity for further exploration within the phenomena of attitudes toward computers, attitude toward e-learning, and overall computer competence.

      In all three of the phenomena being examined, most of the studies reviewed in the literature focused on either the K-12 student population (e.g., Anderson et al., 1980; Bear et al., 1987; Gabriel, 1985; Levine & Donitsa-Schmidt, 1997; Reece & Gable, 1982; Woodrow, 1991), the American college student population (e.g., Delcourt & Kinzie, 1993; Heissen et al., 1987; M. Jones & Pearson, 1996; Karsten & Roth, 1998; Spooner et al., 1999), the international college student population (e.g., Francis & Evans, 1995; Leutner & Weinsier, 1994; Marcoulides, 1991; Pike et al., 1993), or North American teacher population (e.g., Bitter & Davis, 1985; Loyd & Gressard, 1986; Stevens, 1980; Woodrow, 1987). A few of the studies reviewed did use adult subjects from nonacademic settings (e.g., Doll & Torkzadeh, 1988; Harrison & Rainer, 1992; Marcoulides et al., 1995). As noted earlier, it was the author's goal to focus this research study on the corporate adult learner in the hopes of providing more data around adults' perceptions within these phenomena as this population has been neglected in past studies.

      Conflicting results emerged in the literature regarding the correlation between gender and attitudes toward computers and gender and computer literacy. Some studies indicated that males were less anxious or were more computer literate than females (e.g.,

Gabriel, 1985; Griswold, 1983; Koohang, 1986; Loyd & Gressard, 1986; Murphy et al., 1988; Raub, 1981), while other studies did not find significant differences in male and female attitudes toward computers or computer literacy (e.g., Heissen et al., 1987; Koohang, 1989; Pope-Davis & Twig, 1991; Woodrow, 1992, 1994). These conflicting results provided an opportunity to further explore gender differences within the phenomena of attitudes toward computers, computer literacy, and attitudes toward e-learning. These correlations were explored in the author's research study.

The vast majority of the studies reviewed in the literature did find a correlation between amount of computer experience and overall positive attitudes toward computers, amount of computer experience, or both and overall computer literacy (e.g., Gabriel, 1985; Koohang, 1986, 1989; Loyd & Gressard, 1986). However, little data were found to support the correlation between prior e-learning experience and attitudes toward e-learning; Koroghlanian and Brinkerhoff (2000) attempted to look at this relationship, but concluded that "too few cases exist to make statements about this section of the survey" (p. 138). It was within the design of the author's research study to further investigate this relationship to determine if prior e-learning experience or computer experience in general correlates to attitudes toward e-learning.

Most instruments reviewed in the literature that focused on the phenomenon of computer aptitude and self-reported computer competence were antiquated especially given the rapid technological advances in today's society. Many included the subdomain of computer programming skills as a means of identifying computer competence (e.g., Anderson et al., 1980; Gabriel, 1985; Kay, 1993b; Simonson et al., 1987), which may not be a necessary component of computer literacy in the contemporary business environment (Potosky & Bobko, 1998). While incorporating findings from earlier studies, the author of this dissertation developed an instrument to measure computer literacy that fits within the National Center for Educational Statistics' (1983) definition: "whatever a person needs to know and do with computers in order to function competently in our information-based society" (p. 8), while ensuring that it meets today's contemporary business environment.

Although some instruments have been developed to measure attitudes toward e-learning (e.g., Coll Garcia, 2001; Koroghlanian & Brinkerhoff, 2000; Sanders & Morrison-Shetlar, 2001), it remains to be seen whether one will emerge as the standard for measuring attitudes toward technology-enabled learning similar to how the CAS instrument (Loyd & Gressard, 1984) has become one of the most widely used instruments to measure attitudes toward computers. The review of the literature located only one instrument that measures the three phenomenon of attitude toward computers, attitude toward e-learning, and self-reported computer competence (Koroghlanian & Brinkerhoff, 2000), and since its development and initial analysis, no other studies have been found to further validate its reliability and validity. Thus, the author chose to develop an instrument to measure these three phenomena together and look at the relationships they had in helping to determine a subject's overall computer competence and openness to e-learning.

As noted earlier, this research study's goal was to develop a valid and reliable instrument to measure subjects' attitudes toward computers, attitudes toward e-learning, and self-report computer competence. Although this initial instrument development and validation is of extreme importance to training and development leaders, the additional analysis of the data between the independent variables and the results of the instrument are also of interest to those training professionals within the corporate sector. Being able to identify certain demographic variables that may tend to have more positive attitudes toward computers and positive attitude toward e-learning could help corporate leaders identify employees who need or do not need interventions to improve overall attitudes toward these two phenomena. In addition, benchmarking levels of self-reported computer competence could also allow corporate leaders to target needed interventions toward those employees whose computer skills need to be at the company's prescribed basic level.

Chapter Summary

Early investigations into the phenomena of attitudes toward computers began from self-efficacy theory (e.g., Bandura, 1977; Schunk, 1984) as well as exploration in the phenomena of attitudes toward mathematics (e.g., Calvert, 1981; Chisholm, 1980; Fennema, 1977; Fennema & Sherman, 1976). Initially, researchers defined attitudes toward computers simply as computer anxiety (e.g., Heissen et al., 1987; Marcoulides, 1989; McInerney et al., 1999; Simonson et al., 1987), but they eventually broadened this definition beyond the one subdomain of anxiety (e.g., Bear et al., 1987; Kay, 1993a; Loyd & Gressard, 1984; Raub, 1981; Reece & Gable, 1982; Stevens, 1980; Woodrow, 1987).

Like the definition of attitudes toward computers, the phenomenon of computer literacy has developed over time. Although most studies done around computer literacy hold to the broad definition developed by the National Center for Educational Statistics (1983), specific subdomains within this definition have changed as technology has changed. Instruments, such as the MCLAA (Anderson et al., 1980), the CSE (Murphy et al., 1988), and the CAS (Kay, 1993b), all focused on multiple domains of computer literacy but included the subdomain of computer programming as being important to the computer-literate individual. On the contrary, instruments developed by M. Jones and

Pearson (1996) and Potosky and Bobko (1998) omitted computer programming as a

necessary component of the modern, computer-literate individual, showing a shift in the

overall concept of what constitutes computer literacy but is still within the National

Center for Educational Statistics definition. It is interesting to note that measures of

computer literacy have only been in existence for less than 25 years.

Researchers also explored the relationship between attitudes toward computers

and computer literacy. Although some instruments were specifically developed to

measure both phenomena simultaneously in one instrument (e.g., Delcourt & Kinzie,

1993; Kay, 1993a, 1993b), the vast majority of the studies done that looked at the

correlation between computer literacy and attitudes toward computers incorporated the

administration of two separate instruments with each measuring one of the phenomena to

the same population (Roszkowski et al., 1988; Smith & Necessary, 1996; Woodrow,

1992, 1994).

Finally, there is not a large amount of research regarding the measurement of

attitudes toward e-learning as compared to the other phenomena reviewed in the

literature. Initial research done on end-user attitudes toward computer applications can

provide a foundational start to this area of research as e-learning is essentially a software

program used for the purpose of education and learning (Rosenberg, 2001). Doll and

Torkzadeh (1988) developed an instrument whose five components (content, accuracy,

format, ease of use, and timeliness) apply very well to e-learning. Other researchers

purported to measure students' attitudes toward Web-based components of existing

college courses (Spooner et al., 1999). Only two studies reviewed focused on the

development of an instrument looking specifically at attitudes toward multimedia educational delivery (Coll Garcia, 2001; Koroghlanian & Brinkerhoff, 2000).

As noted above, all studies reviewed incorporated a variety of populations within their subjects: K-12 students, American and international college students, North American teachers, and adults working within nonacademic organizations. Based upon these populations and the relationships discovered within the literature, this research explored several hypotheses with which to explore, as noted above.

Chapter 3: Methodology

As noted earlier, this research study focused on the development of a valid and reliable instrument to measure subjects' attitudes toward computers, attitudes toward e-learning, and self-reported computer competence. In addition, the author analyzed pilot study data to explore correlations between these phenomena and certain demographic variables of the pilot study participants. Because the author hoped to determine the status of the phenomena and not administer any treatments to change the phenomena, the approach taken for this research was to utilize a descriptive, quantitative research design, using a single instrument administered to the subjects.

Instrument Development Methodology

The study began with the development of an instrument that measures subjects' attitudes toward computers, attitudes toward e-learning, and self-reported computer competence. The development of this instrument included support for the instrument's validity and reliability. The following section describes how the author developed the instrument.

Participants. The author used a purposive sample for this research study. The purposive sample consisted of individuals who met the following criteria: (a) were at least 18 years of age (an adult as defined in chapter 1) and (b) worked within a corporate or not-for-profit organization that is nonacademic (meaning not in a K-12 or higher education environment). In addition, some participants met at least one of the following additional criteria: (a) worked within the information technology or software fields, (b) were self-professed computer expert, (c) were a self-professed computer novice, (d) rated themselves as possessing high attitudes toward technology-enabled learning, or (e) rated themselves as possessing lower attitudes toward technology-enabled learning. To identify these criteria, the author used the Computer Competence, Attitude, and Behavior Scale (CCABS; Yacovelli, 2004), which the author developed specifically for this research study (see Appendix I). This instrument was specifically used for the validity testing of the Regan CCABS as noted in the Instrument Reliability and Validity section of this chapter.

Instrument development. The newly created instrument is named the Regan CCABS and is comprised of five sections. The version used for this study can be found in Appendix J. The Regan CCABS is an amalgamation of both existing instrument questions and newly developed questions divided into five different sections as follows:

1. Participant demographics. Section 1 of the instrument collects demographic data of the participant. This includes age, gender, United States ZIP code (for potential geographic trending in future studies), and level of educational attainment. In addition, data on current work classification as well as information on number of years within the current business organization are collected. Finally, it also asks if individuals have prior experience with e-learning or technology-enabled learning delivery.

2. Organization demographic. Section 2 collects demographic data about the participant's work organization. These include number of employees within the organization, the type of organization wherein the participant is employed (e.g., government, education, or small business), and the general industry within which the participant's organization is best associated (e.g., manufacturing, retail, travel and hospitality, or information technology). While only some of these data are analyzed for this study, the data could be used for future correlation analysis between certain organizational types and overall employees' attitudes toward computer technology, e-learning, and self-reported computer competence.

3. Self-reported computer competence. Section 3 focuses on the measurement of self-reported computer competence. This section of the instrument is comprised of questions from three instruments: (a) the existing CUES (Potosky & Bobko, 1998), (b) the Regan Technology Behavior Survey developed for this study, and (c) part of the unnamed instrument by Koroghlanian and Brinkerhoff (2000). The CUES, which is comprised of two subscales—the technical competence subscale and general competence subscale—was selected because it met several criteria. First, of all the measures of self-reported computer competence reviewed in the literature, the CUES was determined to be the most contemporary and applicable to today's technological environment; its simplistic 12-question format is contemporary in its verbiage (as opposed to many other instruments developed in the late 1980s and early 1990s that, by today's fast-moving technological standards, seem almost obsolete) and generally reflects current technological trends. Second, its construct validity and reliability had been established by the authors in its initial pilot study (Potosky & Bobko). Finally, subjects used in its initial validity and reliability testing were over 17 years of age (age range 17-60) with the majority (86%) of the participants being between 17 and 36 (Potosky & Bobko), a sample that better reflects the demographics of the subjects that the author used in this research study. Although some questions were slightly modified to be more applicable for use in the corporate environment, this author concurs with the statement made by Potosky and Bobko, the CUES developers, that this instrument is "a convenient, internally consistent measure of overall computer expertise" (p. 384). Permission was obtained to utilize the CUES instrument in the newly developed Regan CCABS.

The Regan Technology Behavior Survey is the name of those collective questions found in Section 3 of the Regan CCABS that were developed by the author for this study.

The focus of these questions is to determine if certain behaviors were indicative of computer knowledge. These questions were developed through observations made by the author while both participating in and facilitating various e-learning sessions in both the corporate and academic environments as well as through consultation of three subject-matter experts whose focus is in technology-enabled learning within a Fortune 50 corporate environment. These questions focused on the demonstration of behaviors that mimic what is generally needed within today's e-learning environment: chat room familiarity, downloading and management of various file types and the utilization and comfort of contemporary technology tools (such as digital pictures, Web-based business transactions, and personal digital assistants).

Finally, Section 3 includes questions from the computer skills section of the unnamed instrument by Koroghlanian and Brinkerhoff (2000). These questions further explore the individual's comfort level around various computer skills, like managing e-mail, locating and installing Web browser plug-ins, and creating and maneuvering through Web pages. These questions were used for two reasons: (a) The questions asked in this section of the instrument were deemed applicable to the corporate, adult learner and reflected the skills the author believes are needed in the contemporary technological business environment, and (b) the Cronbach Alpha of this section was reported at 0.88, indicating a reliable instrument (Koroghlanian & Brinkerhoff, 2000). Some questions were slightly modified to be more applicable for use in the corporate environment. Permission was obtained to utilize this instrument in the newly developed Regan CCABS.

4. Attitudes toward computers. Section 4 of the Regan CCABS focuses on the measurement of attitudes toward computers. Although many instruments exist that

purport to measure this phenomenon (as noted in the review of the literature), the author

chose questions from the existing CAS (Loyd & Gressard, 1984). Many authors have

noted that Loyd and Gressard's Computer Attitude Scale (CAS) is a highly regarded

instrument to measure attitudes toward computers (e.g., Gardner et al., 1993;

Koroghlanian & Brinkerhoff, 2000; Moroz & Nash, 1997b). The four subscales (anxiety,

confidence, liking, and usefulness) are appropriate measures of anxiety and usefulness for

the contemporary, corporate adult learner. In addition to the initial development and

subsequent studies done by its authors (Loyd & Gressard, 1984, 1986; Loyd & Loyd,

1985), the CAS has been analyzed for its reliability and validity extensively by a myriad

of researchers (e.g., Bandalos & Benson, 1990; Christensen & Knezek, 2000; Fennema,

1977; Francis & Evans, 1995; Gardner et al., 1993; Kluever et al., 1994; Roszkowski et

al., 1988; Woodrow, 1991). Although some questions were slightly modified to be more

applicable for use in the contemporary corporate environment, Bandalos and Benson

echoed the author's sentiments as the reason to use this instrument to measure attitudes

toward computers: "The CAS was chosen for this study because it was believed that this

scale, more so than any other instruments available, attempts to define specific

components of computer anxiety" (p. 52). Permission was obtained from the estate of the

author to utilize this instrument in the Regan CCABS.

　　　5. Attitudes toward Internet-delivered training. Section 5 of the Regan CCABS

focuses on the measurement of attitudes toward Internet delivered training, or e-learning.

This section of the instrument is comprised of questions from the unnamed instrument by

Koroghlanian and Brinkerhoff (2000) as well as questions developed by the researcher.

Questions from the section concerning attitudes toward Internet-delivered training

courses from the unnamed instrument by Koroghlanian and Brinkerhoff were chosen because (a) these questions were deemed the most appropriate for adults both familiar with e-learning and those who have not experienced this method of training delivery, (b) this author believes the e-learning strategies being addressed in Koroghlanian and Brinkerhoff's instrument are similar to those within today's corporate learning environment, and (c) the Cronbach Alpha of this section was reported at 0.86, indicating a reliable instrument. Minor revisions to some of the questions from this unnamed instrument were done to make it more applicable in the contemporary corporate environment. In addition to these questions from this unnamed instrument by Koroghlanian and Brinkerhoff, the author included several questions that examine this phenomenon more closely as an attempt to measure participants' attitudes toward e-learning. As indicated earlier, permission was obtained from the author to utilize this instrument in the newly-developed Regan CCABS.

The scoring methodology for the Regan CCABS uses a 5-point Likert scale with the following breakdown: SD = *strongly disagree*, D = *disagree*, DA = *sometimes disagree/agree*, A = *agree*, and SA = *strongly agree*. Sections 1 and 2 are not scored as they are focused on demographic data of the participants and their respective organizations. In Section 3 (self-reported computer competence), item responses are coded so that the higher score corresponds to a higher degree of self-reported computer knowledge. Scores for this scale, which includes the CUES (Potosky & Bobko, 1998), the Regan Technology Behavior Survey, and the subscale of computer skill from the unnamed instrument by Koroghlanian and Brinkerhoff (2000), can range from 40 to 200 with a higher score indicative of higher self-reported computer knowledge.

In Section 4 (attitudes toward computers), item responses are coded so that the higher score corresponds to a higher degree of liking, confidence, or perception of usefulness and a lower degree of anxiety toward computers (Loyd & Gressard, 1984).

This section of the instrument is based upon the CAS (Loyd & Gressard, 1984) and

includes additional questions the author developed to further measure this particular

phenomena. The total score for this particular scale of the Regan CCABS would range

from 50 to 250, and similar to Loyd and Gressard's (1984) scoring methodology, the

higher the score is indicative of a more positive attitude toward computers.

In Section 5 (attitudes toward e-learning), item responses are coded so that the

higher score corresponds to a more positive attitude toward Internet-delivered training (or

e-learning). Based upon the initial survey developed for this study, 14 of the 30 questions

in Section 5 were negatively stated so scoring was reverse coded in order to maintain a

higher score indicating a more positive attitude toward e-learning. Scores in this section

of the Regan CCABS range from 30 to 150.

As an analysis point, participants were given two ways in which to complete the

Regan CCABS, either in paper form or via the Internet. Although all participants were

given the paper form of the instrument, the introductory letter also indicated a Web

address where the participants could complete the survey. The only difference between

the two versions of the instrument was the final qualitative question, "when given the

choice, I choose to take this survey [on paper or via the Internet, depending on the

delivery format selected] because . . . " This selection was then correlated with the overall

subscales of attitude toward computers and self-reported computer competence (as

indicated in the validity and reliability section, below).

Reliability and validity analysis. Before an instrument can be used in any research

study, its reliability and validity must be determined (American Psychological

Association, 1985). According to Popham (1993), reliability "refers to the consistency with which a measure assesses whatever it is measuring" (p. 120). Leedy and Ormrod (2001) noted that validity is "the extent to which the instrument measures what it is supposed to measure" (p. 98). Thus, the establishment of the reliability and validity for the Regan CCABS was paramount for this research study.

Reliability analysis on the Regan CCABS focused on the notion that reliability is a necessary but not sufficient condition for validity (Popham, 1993; Tull & Albaum, 1973) and that validity is affected by reliability. The author assessed the reliability of the instrument first, then its validity. A reliable instrument produces the same results when given to either the same sample or a different sample of the same size from a given population (American Psychological Association, 1985; Leedy & Ormrod, 2001; Popham; Ravid, 2000; Tull & Albaum); thus, when an instrument is reliable, differences in results can be attributed to actual differences in respondents rather than to random causes (Popham; Tull & Albaum). The author gathered evidence to support the overall reliability of the newly created instrument and, therefore, strove for a high coefficient of reliability for the three measured subscales of the Regan CCABS. According to Gable (1986), reliability figures of above 0.70 are acceptable levels for an attitude measure.

Although several methods exist for the establishment of reliability of an instrument (Leedy & Ormrod, 2001; Ravid, 2000; Tull & Albaum, 1973), the author used two tactics to support the overall reliability of the instrument. First, the author conducted a test-retest scenario on a sample of those who participate in the overall study. In this method, the subjects took the instrument and then were given the same instrument after a period of time; theoretically, if the instrument is reliable, the scores between the two administrations should be relatively close (Popham, 1993; Tull & Albaum). The author ensured that at least 7 to 10 days elapsed between administrations of the instrument.

Coefficients of reliability were determined between these administrations of the instrument as reported in chapter 4.

The second tactic to support the instrument's overall reliability that was used was the split-half technique. In this tactic, the Regan CCABS was evenly distributed into two instruments, and the two subscores for each section were correlated with the resulting correlation coefficients considered to be an estimate of the degree to which the two halves of the instrument would measure the phenomena in question consistently (Popham, 1993; Tull & Albaum, 1973). Tull and Albaum suggested having at least 16 to 20 items in each scale in order to use the split-half approach, and the current version of the Regan CCABS met this criterion with 40, 50, and 30 items in each of the three measured subscales, respectively. These two tactics should adequately provide evidence to support the overall reliability of the Regan CCABS.

The validity analysis of the Regan CCABS focused on the definition of validity according to the American Psychological Association (1985). As stated in the *Standards for Educational and Psychological Testing* (American Psychological Association), there are three types of validity: content validity, criterion-related validity, and construct validity A fourth type of validity, face validity, is also mentioned by several authors as a means of helping to establish the overall validity for an instrument (Leedy & Ormrod, 2001; Ravid, 2000). It was the author's intent to establish support in all four types of validity for this new instrument.

The face validity of the instrument was assessed by the author and select subject-matter experts familiar with educational evaluation and measurement. Face validity refers to the degree to which the instrument appears to measure the intended phenomenon (Leedy & Ormrod, 2001; Ravid, 2000). Although face validity is not part of the standards mentioned in the *Standards for Educational and Psychological Testing* (American Psychological Association, 1985), Ravid noted that the establishment of face validity can affect how well the instrument is accepted and used in the field. In addition, Ravid stated face validity can also help motivate those completing the instrument, because "they can see the relevancy of the test to the perceived task" (p. 268). The use of face validity in addition to other types of validity helped to support the overall validity of the instrument (Leedy & Ormrod).

Content validity is the degree to which an instrument is a representative sample of the content area (or domain) being measured (American Psychological Association, 1985; Leedy & Ormrod, 2001; Ravid, 2000). As Tull and Albaum (1973) suggested, the review by subject-matter experts is one tactic for establishing an instrument's content validity. The author enlisted the assistance of four subject-matter experts to establish the content validity of the instrument. These included experts in the fields of instructional technology, instrument and assessment design, communications, and corporate learning strategy. These subject-matter experts were asked to review the instrument to ensure that it measures the phenomena intended as defined by the author (attitude toward computers, attitude toward e-learning, and self-reported computer competence). Furthermore, the questions in the instrument were reviewed for their clarity and objectivity so there was little chance for subjective interpretation. The credibility of these four subject-matter experts are as follows:

1. The first subject-matter expert is associate professor of communications at a small liberal arts college in Central Florida. In addition to a wide range of consulting with business organizations regarding training and leadership development, this subject-matter expert's area of research focus includes communication among learners and teachers in a

distance environment.

2. The second subject-matter expert has worked for several years within a Fortune 50 company's training and development area, focusing on instrument development and training assessment. This subject-matter expert's specialty is the assessment of corporate learners using a variety of surveying methods from paper-based to electronic delivery. His forte is in learner needs assessment.

3. The third subject-matter expert is leader of a market research organization for a large Fortune 50 company. This subject-matter expert's area of expertise is instrument development, qualitative and quantitative research methodologies for the business environment, and the strategic use of these data to advance business goals and objectives.

4. The fourth subject-matter expert is a senior partner at a Fortune 50 technology and consulting company whose focus is in learning and development for some of the largest companies in the world. This subject-matter expert's area of expertise includes the development and implementation of enterprise learning strategy and the incorporation of technology to accomplish the overall training goals for large organizations.

Together, these subject-matter experts represent over 65 years of experience in education, training, and marketing fields. The feedback form used by the subject matter experts can be found in Appendix K.

Construct validity refers to the extent to which an instrument measures and provides accurate information about a theoretical trait or characteristic (American Psychological Association, 1985; Leedy & Ormrod, 2001; Ravid, 2000). Kerlinger (1986) noted that one effective tactic to establish an instrument's construct validity is through the correlations among total scores and item scores. The first tactic the author used to support the instrument's overall construct validity was to look at the overall correlations among the scores of each of the three measured subscales of the instrument (self-reported computer competence, attitudes toward computers, and attitudes toward e-learning) and their correlation among each of the items listed in the three subsections.

The second tactic the author used to support the construct validity of the Regan CCABS was through comparison of purposive subjects and their scores on the three subscales of the instrument. For Section 3 (self-reported computer competence), the author compared the results of the instrument to subjects whose self-reported level of computer competence is known to be higher, based upon information provided in the CCABS (Yacovelli, 2004; see Appendix I). Theoretically, subjects whose self-reported computer knowledge is higher should obtain a higher score on Section 3 of the newly established instrument (Tull & Albaum, 1973). In Section 4 (attitudes toward computers), the author administered the instrument to subjects whose attitude toward computers is known to be more positive or more negative. Similarly, subjects whose attitude towards computers is lower should score relatively low on this section of the instrument; conversely, those whose attitude toward computers is high should score relatively higher on the newly established instrument. Similar to the approach taken for Section 4, to support the construct validity for Section 5 (attitudes toward e-learning), the author administered the instrument to subjects whose attitude toward e-learning is known to be more positive or more negative, respectively (as measured by the CCABS instrument). Theoretically, subjects whose attitude towards e-learning is low should score relatively low on this section of the instrument; conversely, those whose attitude toward e-learning is high should score relatively higher on the newly established instrument.

Finally, criterion-related validity refers to the extent to which the performance of an instrument of measurement correlates with another well-established instrument that purports to measure the same phenomenon (American Psychological Association, 1985; Leedy & Ormrod, 2001; Ravid, 2000). Similar to the approach taken by many of the authors reviewed in the literature (e.g., Christensen & Knezek, 2000; Francis & Evans, 1995; Gressard & Loyd, 1985; Harrison & Rainer, 1992; Kluever et al., 1994; Reece & Gable, 1982; Roszkowski et al., 1988; Simonson et al., 1987; Woodrow, 1991, 1994), the author used the tactic of correlating the results of various aspects of the three subscales of the Regan CCABS with existing instruments whose validity and reliability have been established. Because the author used both established instruments in creating new questions to measure the same phenomena, comparison of the data collected between the author's measures and existing measures helped ascertain the instrument's construct validity.

For Section 3 (self-reported computer competence), the author examined the correlation coefficients of the Computer Attitude and Experience Scale (Potosky & Bobko, 1998), which are Questions 12-19, 25, 29, 33, and 34 in the newly developed Regan CCABS, and compared these scores to the overall subscore of this section of the instrument. This also was done with the questions garnered from the unnamed instrument by Koroghlanian and Brinkerhoff (2000), which are Questions 35-47 of the Regan CCABS and the subscore of Section 3 of the Regan CCABS. For Section 4 (attitudes toward computers) of the newly developed instrument, the author performed the same analysis by comparing the correlation coefficients of the CAS (Loyd & Gressard, 1984; Questions 51-90 of the Regan CCABS) and the overall subscore of this section of the instrument. And for Section 5 (attitudes toward e-learning), the subscores for this section can be compared to the questions acquired from the unnamed instrument by Koroghlanian and Brinkerhoff (2000; Questions 101-118 of the Regan CCABS).

Through these tactics and strategies the author believes to have provided ample data to support the Regan CCABS's face, content, construct, and criterion-related validity. Table 1 summarizes these tactics to gather data that support the overall reliability and validity of the developed instrument.

Finally, this research study also looked at correlations between key demographics collected from subjects and their responses to the three subscales incorporated within the Regan CCABS. Although this analysis is not intended to be representative of the greater North American corporate adult learner, the author hoped to explore several areas to see if trends from previous studies were supported or refuted.

Table 1

Summary of Reliability and Validity Methodology

Step	Actions
Gathering data to support the overall reliability of the Regan CCABS	1. Test-retest scenario using a subsample of participants.
	2. Split-half technique on the scores from all participants.
Gathering data to support the overall validity of Regan CCABS	3. Face validity of the instrument, using feedback from subject matter experts and the author.
	4. Content validity of the instrument, using feedback from subject matter experts and the author.
	5. Construct validity of the instrument, using two tactics: (a) analysis of correlation statistics between each item of the instrument and its overall score; and (b) analysis of correlation statistics of purposive subjects.
	6. Criterion-related validity of the instrument using correlation statistics between existing instruments and the newly created instrument.

Discussion

The primary end user for the instrument developed is training and development professionals within the corporate and not-for-profit sectors. Once data were gathered to support the instrument's overall reliability and validity, these professionals could use this instrument in their initial needs analysis for training interventions. Armed with the data collected on their individual employees, training managers could easily benchmark their target audiences' attitudes toward computers, attitudes toward e-learning, and self-reported computer competence. These data could be used to develop interventions for employees prior to using computers for training delivery, thus saving the company time and money regarding the implementation of training solutions.

Limitations to the instrument. There are limitations to the instrument. First, as noted earlier in the literature, the instrument was being developed for use by corporate, adult learners and may not be appropriate for use with populations such as the K-12 students, traditional-aged college students, or adults working in a noncorporate organization (such as academia). Although it is the author's hope that this instrument is universally acceptable for succinctly measuring computer attitude, attitudes toward e-learning, and self-reported computer competence, it was beyond the scope of this study to validate and test the reliability of the instrument on nonadult, noncorporate learners.

The development of the instrument was for North American business personnel, and a secondary limitation may be using the instrument beyond a North American audience. It was beyond the scope of this examination to determine if the instrument developed is valid and reliable to other non-North American audiences (such as Asian, European, or South American audiences).

Finally, the technological advances within our society have rapidly changed over the past few years, greatly impacting the way we live and how we learn. Like other instruments developed that focus on the measurement of computer literacy or competence as well as attitudes toward computer technology, there is a limited shelf life around this type of measurement due to the rapid advances of technology. An additional limitation to this instrument would be the potential limited time usage that the instrument could be employed. Although the author believes that the phenomenon of attitudes toward computers is less impacted by specific computer advances, self-reported computer competence is contingent upon the current technological trends, and e-learning methodology being utilized today (and measured in the newly developed instrument) may be obsolete tomorrow. Like other instruments before that have attempted to measure computer competence, technological advances will eventually make the facet of the instrument focused on self-reported computer competence obsolete, making it necessary to update and revalidate the instrument as new questions more appropriate to current technology trends are incorporated into the instrument.

Delimitations to the instrument. In addition to the limitations listed above, delimitations to the proposed research study should be noted. First, although the instrument being developed has an extensive demographic section (see Appendix J) and this information will potentially be beneficial for future studies that utilize the Regan CCABS, it was not the author's intent to analyze the attitudes toward computers, attitudes toward e-learning, or the self-reported computer competence of participants with some of the demographic variables being collected. Specifically, variables of ZIP code, number of years the participants have been with their current business organization, or data on current hourly or salaried work classification were not analyzed in the research study. In addition, although much of the demographic data could be analyzed in concert with existing data from the United States 2000 Census (U.S. Census Bureau Public Information Office, 2002), it was not the intent of the study to analyze the information collected from participants with existing data from the 2000 United States Census.

Although the instrument did collect information regarding the participants' current organization, it was not the intent of this author to analyze these data for trends or correlations between other variables being collected within the proposed study. For example, data on number of employees within the organization, the type of organization wherein the participant is employed (e.g., government, education, small business), and the industry within which the participant's organization is best associated were collected but not analyzed at this time. However, these data could be used for future correlation analysis between certain organizational types and overall employees' attitudes toward computer technology, e-learning, and self-reported computer competence.

Materials. The implementation of this study required minimal materials. Participants received the paper version of the Regan CCABS. This instrument was comprised of five sections: (a) participant demographics, (b) organization demographics, (c) self-reported computer competence, (d) attitudes toward computers, and (e) attitudes toward Internet-delivered training. The instrument is an amalgamation of both existing instrument questions and newly developed questions.

In addition to the paper version of the Regan CCABS, participants also received a piece of paper with the Internet address for the electronic version of the Regan CCABS (available at http://www.topdoglearning.biz/survey). Participants' choice in delivery was an analysis point for the study.

Procedure. The specific procedures employed in this research study were as follows:

1. The author enlisted the assistance of key individuals (here after referred to as research representatives) at each organization who disseminated and collected the necessary paperwork. These individuals were personal contacts of the researcher, and

they received both verbal and written instructions as to how to disseminate and collect the required paperwork in a confidential manner. An attempt was be made to enlist the assistance of research representatives from a diverse number of business and not-for-profit settings for this study.

2. Organization consent forms were procured from each organization participating in the study via the research representative. No surveys were distributed to an organization unless the organizational consent form was on file.

3. The author delivered the following items to each research representative: (a) a supply of the paper version of the Regan CCABS, (b) a supply of the Participant Consent Forms, (c) a supply of sealable envelopes for participants and (d) instructions for disseminating and collecting the materials to participants. It is important to note that each organization participating in the study was assigned a lot number in order to track response rates at each individual organization. The lot number was in no way indicative of the individual participant, only their affiliated organization.

4. The research representative distributed three items to each participant: (a) the paper version of the Regan CCABS, (b) a sealable envelope, and (c) a Participant Consent Form. The consent form included the normal verbiage required for consent forms, but it also included the Internet address for the electronic version of the Regan CCABS should participants wish to complete the survey electronically. It also identified the organizational lot number.

5. Participants chose to complete either the paper version of the Regan CCABS or the electronic version of the same instrument. Participants then returned the paper version of the Regan CCABS (regardless of which version they choose to use) in the sealed envelope along with the signed Participant Consent Form to the research representative.

6. The research representative returned the documents to the author. The overall timeframe for data collection entailed 2 weeks from distribution of surveys to the receipt of completed surveys.

7. The author entered both paper and electronic responses from participants into SPSS 11.5 statistical data analysis software.

Table 2 summarizes these tactics used to gather data in the research study.

Table 2

Summary of Implementation Procedure

Step	Actions
Solicited and coordinated study at various corporate sites that participated in the study.	1. The author enlisted the assistance of research representatives at each organization that disseminated and collected the necessary paperwork.
	2. Organization consent forms were procured from each organization participating in the study.
	3. The author delivered a supply of the following items to each research representative: (a) paper versions of the Regan CCABS, (b) Participant Consent Forms, (c) sealable envelopes, and (d) instructions for disseminating and collecting the materials to participants.
Disseminated items to subjects.	4. The research representative distributed three items to each participant: (a) the paper version of the Regan CCABS, (b) sealable envelope, and (c) a Participant Consent Form. The overall timeframe for data collection was 2 weeks from distribution of surveys to the receipt of completed surveys.
Collected data from subjects.	5. Participants completed either the paper version or the electronic version of the instrument. Participants returned the paper version of the Regan CCABS (in a sealable envelope) and the signed Participant Consent Form to the research representative.
	6. The research representative returned the documents to the author.
Analyzed data from subjects.	7. The author entered both paper responses and electronic responses into SPSS 11.5 statistical data analysis software.

Note. CCABS = Computer Competence, Attitude, and Behavior Scale.

Results

As noted earlier in the literature, the author investigated six hypotheses during the development of this new instrument. The six hypotheses are as follows:

1. Subjects' attitudes toward computers will be positively correlated with their attitude toward e-learning as a method of learning. This hypothesis was tested using the data gathered from Section 4: Attitudes Toward Computers and Section 5: Attitudes Toward Internet-Delivered Training of the Regan CCABS.

2. Subjects' age will be negatively correlated with self-reported computer competence. This hypothesis was tested using the data gathered from Section 1: Participant Demographics and Section 3: Self-Reported Computer Competence of the Regan CCABS.

3. Subjects' age will be negatively correlated with attitudes toward e-learning. This hypothesis was tested using the data gathered from Section 1: Participant Demographics and 5: Attitudes Toward Internet-Delivered Training of the Regan CCABS.

4. Subjects' level of education will be positively correlated with their attitudes toward e-learning. Like Hypothesis 3, this hypothesis was tested using the data gathered from Section 1: Participant Demographics and 5: Attitudes Toward Internet-Delivered Training of the Regan CCABS.

5. Subjects' self-reported computer competence will be positively correlated with overall attitudes toward e-learning. This hypothesis was tested using the data gathered from Section 3: Self-Reported Computer Competence and Section 5: Attitudes Toward Internet-Delivered Training of the Regan CCABS.

6. There will be no significant difference between gender and attitudes toward computers, attitudes toward technology-enabled learning, and self-reported computer competence. This hypothesis was tested using the data gathered from Section 1:

Participant Demographics in concert with Section 3: Self-Reported Computer Competence, Section 4: Attitudes Toward Computers, and Section 5: Attitudes Toward Internet-Delivered Training, respectively, of the Regan CCABS.

Chapter Summary

This research study focused on the development of a valid and reliable instrument to measure subjects' attitudes toward computers, attitudes toward e-learning, and self-reported computer competence. In tandem with this, the author also analyzed these phenomena and their correlation with various demographic variables of the participants of the study. In this chapter, the author described the methodology used in order to develop said instrument and ensure its validity and reliability.

The newly developed instrument was named the Regan CCABS. This instrument consists of five sections: (a) Participant Demographics, (b) Organization Demographics, (c) Self-Reported Computer Competence, (d) Attitudes Toward Computers, and (e) Attitudes Toward Internet-Delivered Training. Each section is comprised of entirely new questions for this research or a combination of existing instruments whose validity and reliability have been explored extensively in previous studies and newly created questions by the author. Each section is scored so that higher scores are indicative of more positive attitudes or higher competence. Participants also had the option of either completing the instrument via paper or they could opt to complete the instrument via the Internet, which in itself was an analysis point for the research study.

The subjects who participated in the study were comprised of both purposive sampling (in conjunction with the validity testing of the newly created instrument) and convenience sampling for the initial distribution of the instrument. Subjects met two simple criteria: (a) were at least 18 years of age (thus constituted as adults) and (b) worked within a corporate or not-for-profit organization that is nonacademic (meaning not K-12 or higher education environments). In addition, a small subsample of subjects met additional criteria for helping to establish the instrument's overall validity and reliability. An attempt was made to obtain subjects from several different vocational settings, totaling 144 subjects for the study.

Validity and reliability were paramount to this research study. The author used two tactics to support the overall reliability of the Regan CCABS. First, the author conducted a test-retest scenario on a sample of those who participated in the overall study. Second, a split-half technique was used when analyzing the results of the initial pilot study. These two tactics adequately provided evidence to support the overall reliability of the instrument.

It was the author's intent to establish support for all four types of validity for this new instrument. To support the instrument's overall face validity, the author reviewed the instrument as well as enlisted the assistance of four subject-matter experts. These included experts in the field of instructional technology, instrument and assessment design, communications, and corporate learning strategy. Second, to establish the content validity of the instrument, these same subject-matter experts were asked to review the instrument to ensure that it measured the phenomena intended (attitude toward computers, attitude toward e-learning, and self-reported computer competence) and to review the instrument to ensure objectivity. Third, to support the instrument's overall construct validity, the author looked at the overall correlations between the scores of each of the three measured subscales of the instrument (self-reported computer competence, attitudes toward computers, and attitudes toward e-learning) and their correlation between each of the items listed in the subsections. In addition, the author used a purposive sample to analyze their scores on the three subscales of the instrument. Finally, to support the overall criterion-related validity of the Regan CCABS, the author used the tactic of correlating the results of various aspects of the three subscales of the instrument with existing instruments whose validity and reliability have been established.

Once data to support the overall validity and reliability of the instrument were established, the author explored several hypotheses during the study, including whether or not subjects' attitudes toward computers overall would correlate with their attitude toward e-learning as a method of learning. It was hypothesized that, while subjects would possess an overall positive attitude toward computers, they would tend to hold a low level of self-reported computer competence. In addition, it was hypothesized that there would be a correlation between age and computer skill as those participants who are older would tend to have lower self-reported computer competence than their younger counterparts among other demographic variable correlations to attitudes toward computers and attitudes toward e-learning. These findings are explored in chapter 4.

Limitations existed for this study. As noted earlier, the newly developed instrument was used by corporate, adult learners and thus may not be appropriate for usage with other populations such as K-12 students, college students, or adults working within an academic environment. This study was conducted on a group of North American business personnel, and a secondary limitation was using the instrument beyond a North American audience. Finally, like other instruments developed that focus on the measurement of attitudes toward computer technology, there is a limited shelf life around this type of measurement due to the rapid advances of technology within our information-based society.

Regarding the delimitations to this study, it was not the author's intention to analyze certain demographic variables that were collected in the Regan CCABS and the participants' results of the instrument. In addition, it was not the author's intention to analyze the information collected from participants with existing data from the 2000 U.S. Census. Finally, although certain variables were collected regarding the participants' affiliated business organization, it was not the author's intention to analyze these data for trends or correlations between other variables being collected within this research study; however, these data may be used for future analyses.

Chapter 4: Results

Introduction

This research study focused on the development of a valid and reliable instrument

to measure three phenomena: subjects' attitudes toward computers, their attitudes toward

e-learning, and their self-reported computer competence. Because the author wished to

determine the status of the phenomena and not administer any treatments to change the

phenomena, the approach taken for this research plan was to utilize a descriptive,

quantitative research design, using a single instrument administered to the subjects. This

chapter describes the results of the implementation of the research described in chapter 3,

including the types of statistical analysis used to help establish the instrument's validity

and reliability.

Instrument Validation

Subjects. A total of 144 individuals participated in the research study. These

individuals were from four organizations, which were all nonacademic entities (business

and government agencies). All individuals were over the age of 18 years old. Participants

were all volunteers within the research study.

Demographic data and descriptive statistics. There was a close balance between

male and female subjects in this research study (female $n = 82$, or 56.9% of the total

sample; male $n = 62$, 43.1%). Males scored slightly higher in both Section 3: self-

reported computer competence ($M = 4.22$) and Section 4: Attitudes Toward Computers

($M = 4.29$), but females scored slightly higher with regard to Section 5: Attitudes Toward

e-Learning ($M = 3.80$). Table 3 displays the descriptive statistics by gender.

All participants were over the age of 18 with the largest percentage (43.0%, $n =$

62) between the ages of 30 and 39. Only 14.6% of participants were over 50 years of age.

Table 4 displays the frequencies of age categories for the participants.

Table 3

Descriptive Statistics by Gender for the Regan CCABS

Subscore section	N		M		SD		SEM	
	M	F	M	F	M	F	M	F
Self-reported computer competence	62	82	4.22	3.88	0.54	0.64	0.07	0.07
Attitudes toward computers	62	82	4.29	4.23	0.49	.052	0.06	0.06
Attitudes toward e-learning	62	82	3.76	3.80	0.57	0.66	0.07	0.07

Note. CCABS = Computer Competence, Attitude, and Behavior Scale (Yacovelli, 2004); M = male, F = female.

Sixty-seven percent of participants were college educated, possessing at least an associate's degree ($n = 97$), and 68% of the participants ($n = 98$) identified themselves as being salaried workers (while 27% classified themselves as hourly). Table 5 shows the frequencies of educational attainment.

Regarding experience with computers, over half (66%) of the participants ($n = 95$) reported having taken an Internet-delivered course, and almost all (97%; $n = 140$) reported owning a computer. As measured by Section 3: Self-Reported Computer Competence of the Regan CCABS, subjects possessed a relatively high level of computer competence (*high* was defined by the author as being above the 50th percentile), and the mean score for Section 3 of the Regan CCABS for the participants in this research study ($N = 144$) was 4.03 ($SD = 0.62$) with a range in scores being 1.18 to 5.00.

Table 4

Responder Age Breakdown

Age range	Frequency	Percentage	Cumulative percentage
18-29	28	19.50	19.5
30-39	62	43.00	62.50
40-49	33	22.90	85.40
50-59	19	13.20	98.60
60-75	2	1.40	100.00

Of all participants, a minority (37.50%, $n = 54$) chose to take the instrument via paper, citing reasons such as "convenience," "no Internet or computer access" at the time of taking the instrument, and the "ability to manage interruptions" while taking the instrument. The remaining 62.50% ($n = 90$) chose to complete the survey via the Internet, citing reasons such as "convenience to their current location," easy and "speed of entry," and neater or "more legible responses" than the paper version. Using an independent samples *t* test, no significant difference between subjects' selection of media for completing the survey (paper based or via the Internet) for any of the three phenomena being observed in the Regan CCABS ($p < 0.01$). Table 6 displays data regarding instrument delivery method and the subscores for the Regan CCABS.

Finally, relative to the scale presented in Section 4: Attitudes Toward Computers of the Regan CCABS, participants of this research study possessed positive attitudes toward computers. *Positive* was defined by this author as having a mean score at or above 4.00. The mean score for Section 4 of the Regan CCABS for the participants in this research study ($N = 144$) was 4.25 ($SD = 0.51$) with a range in scores being 2.58 to 5.00.

Table 5

Responder Education Attainment Levels

Level of education	Frequency	Percentage	Cumulative percentage
11th to 12th grade without high school diploma	1	0.70	0.70
High school diploma or equivalent	12	8.30	9.00
Some college credit but less than 1 year	15	10.40	19.40
1 or more years of college but no degree	19	13.20	32.60
Associate degree	11	7.60	40.20
Bachelor degree	58	40.30	80.50
Master degree	18	12.50	93.00
Professional degree	8	5.60	98.60
Doctorate degree	2	1.40	100.00

Procedure. All participants received three items: (a) the Participant Consent Form, (b) a sealable envelope, and (c) a paper version of the Regan CCABS. Both the Participant Consent Form and the paper version of the instrument included the Internet address of the electronic version of the same survey should participants wish to complete the survey electronically as opposed to via paper. In addition, 25 participants received the CCABS (Yacovelli, 2004) in addition to the Regan CCABS. Seven subjects agreed to retake the survey after a period of time had elapsed in order to analyze test-retest data.

The study was conducted over a 2-week period.

Table 6

Correlations Between Instrument Delivery and the Three Subscales of the Regan CCABS

Regan CCABS section subscore	F	Sig.	*t*	*df*	Sig. (2-tailed)	Mean difference	*SE* difference	95% confidence interval of difference	
								Lower	Upper
Self-reported computer competence	1.59	0.21	2.05	142	0.042	0.43	0.21	0.02	0.85
Attitudes toward computers	0.10	0.75	1.44	142	0.152	0.25	0.17	-0.09	0.59
Attitudes toward e-learning	0.24	0.62	1.05	142	0.300	0.22	0.21	-0.20	0.65

t test for equality of means

Note. CCABS = Computer Competence, Attitude, and Behavior Survey; equal variances assumed for Levene's Test for Equality of Variances.

Data were then entered into SPSS Statistical Software (Version 11.5) for analysis. Responses were converted into numeric values (*strongly disagree* = 1, *disagree* = 2, *sometimes disagree/agree* = 3, *agree* = 4, and *strongly agree* = 5), while the 39 negatively worded questions (52, 53, 56, 57, 60, 63, 64, 66, 67, 69, 72, 74, 76, 78, 80, 82, 85, 86, 88, 90, 91, 95, 96, 99, 100, 102, 105, 107, 109, 111, 114, 115, 118, 119, 121, 124, 125, 126, and 130) were reverse coded (*strongly disagree* = 5, *disagree* = 4, *sometimes disagree/agree* = 3, *agree* = 2, and *strongly agree* = 1). Variables to subtotal tabulation for each of the three subscales of the instrument were added to the database, providing a mean score of the overall subsection. For the instrument, the higher the score, the more positive the attitudes toward computers and e-learning and the higher the self-reported computer competence.

Validity analysis of the Regan CCABS. As noted earlier in the dissertation, the author followed several procedures to gather data to support four types of validity: face, content, construct, and criterion related (American Psychological Association, 1985; Leedy, 2001; Ravid, 2000).

The face validity of the instrument was assessed by the author and four select subject-matter experts familiar with educational evaluation and measurement and the three phenomena being examined in the instrument. As described in chapter 3, these included an associate professor of communications at a small liberal arts college in Central Florida with a background in effective electronic communication methodologies; a leader within a Fortune 50 company's training and development area, focusing on instrument development and training assessment; a leader of a market research organization for a large Fortune 50 company with expertise is instrument development, and qualitative and quantitative research methodologies for the business environment; and a senior partner at a Fortune 50 technology and consulting company whose focus is in learning and development for some of the largest companies in the world. As the developer of the instrument, the author reviewed its face validity at the time of its creation, ensuring that both existing questions from previous surveys and newly developed questions appeared to measure the three phenomena. Subject-matter experts were given a form to complete, asking them to write their comments regarding the instrument's face validity: specifically if the instrument looked as if it measured the three phenomenon intended. All subject-matter experts agreed that, upon first examination, the three sections of the Regan CCABS did indeed address the three phenomena in question.

To examine the instrument's content validity, subject-matter experts were specifically asked to respond to the following questions on the form for each of the three phenomena being measured by the newly created instrument: "In your opinion, is this instrument a representative sample of the domain of . . ." Using a scale where 1 indicates *does not seem to contain a representative sample of the domain* and 10 indicates *seems to accurately contain a representative sample of the domain*, subject-matter experts rated the instrument's perceived content validity as to whether the survey measured the three phenomena (self-reported computer competence, attitudes toward computers, and attitudes toward e-learning). For Section 3, subject-matter experts selected a mean score of 8.75 ($SD = 0.5$); one subject-matter expert noted, "This section shows a broad continuum of skills to help determine the respondents' competence." Section 4 received a mean score of 9 ($SD = 0.82$) from the subject-matter experts with one subject-matter expert noting, "This section [Section 4] seems to reflect emotion and feelings regarding computers." Finally, similar to Section 3, subject-matter experts selected a mean score for Section 5 of 8.75 ($SD = 0.5$). Table 7 provides the detailed ratings from the subject-matter experts for the three sections of the instrument and their content validity.

It is also important to note that subject-matter experts were asked to critique each individual item as it related to the three sections and help ascertain the item's clarity of intent and objectivity. Their formative feedback was incorporated into the survey's development, was used for the research study, and contributed to the instrument's overall content validity.

Two strategies were chosen to collect data to support the instrument's overall construct validity. First, the author looked at the overall correlations between the scores of each of the three measured subscales of the instrument (self-reported computer competence, attitudes toward computers, and attitudes toward e-learning) and their

correlation between each of the individual items comprising the three subsections.

Table 7

Subject-Matter Experts' Content Validity Feedback

Subject-matter expert	Self-reported computer competence	Attitudes toward computers	Attitudes toward e-learning
1	8	9	9
2	8	9	9
3	9	8	8
4	9	10	9

Note. The question was, "In your opinion, is this instrument a representative sample of the domain of ..." 1 = *does not seem to contain a representative sample of the domain;* 10 = *seems to accurately contain a representative sample of the domain.*

In Section 3: Self-Reported Computer Competence, of the 40 items that comprise this section of the instrument, 35 (or 87.5% of all items) realized a correlation coefficient at or above 0.50, with the highest coefficient being 0.81 (Question 50, "Overall, I would consider myself to be competent with computers"). All 40 items were significant at the 0.01 level (two tailed). The five items that did not realize this level of correlation are listed in Table 8, which centered around writing computer programs, using mainframe computers, using an automated teller machine (ATM) and personal digital assistant (PDA), and reading computer literature frequently. A complete listing of all the items for Section 3 and their Pearson correlation coefficients and significance levels can be found in Appendix O.

Table 8

Item-to-Subtotal Correlation: Items With Low Correlation Coefficients for Section 3: Self-Reported Computer Competence

Question no.	Question	Pearson correlation	Two-tailed significance
16	I know how to write computer programs.	.36*	0.000
18	I often use a mainframe computer system.	.24*	0.004
30	I have used an automated teller machine.	.38*	0.000
32	I use a Palm Pilot or other type of personal digital assistant frequently.	.30*	0.000
33	I frequently read computer magazines or other sources of information that describe new computer technology.	.49*	0.000

Note. *Correlation is significant at the 0.01 level (two tailed).

In Section 4: Attitudes Toward Computers, of the 50 items within this section of the instrument 42 (or 84%) of the items within the section achieved a correlation coefficient of 0.51 or higher with the highest coefficient being 0.84 (Question 70, "I have a lot of self-confidence when it comes to working with computers"). All 50 items were significant at the 0.01 level (two tailed). The 8 items that did not achieve this level of correlation are listed in Table 9, and a complete listing of all the items for Section 4 and their Pearson correlation coefficients and significance levels can be found in Appendix P.

In Section 5: Attitudes Toward e-Learning, of the 30 items within this section of the instrument, all but one (or 96.67%) of the items within the section achieved a correlation coefficient of 0.51 or higher with the highest coefficient being 0.84 (Question

112, "I would be excited to take a training class delivered over the Internet"). All 30

items were significant at the 0.01 level (two tailed). Question 106, "I feel at ease using

the Internet (or 'Web')," achieved a coefficient of 0.36. A complete listing of all the

items for Section 5 and their Pearson correlation coefficients and significance levels can

be found in Appendix Q.

Table 9

Item-to-Subtotal Correlation: Items With Low Correlation Coefficients for Section 4: Attitudes Toward Computers

Question no.	Question	Pearson correlation	Two-tailed significance
52	I get anxious when I think of trying to use a computer.	.46*	0.000
53	I'm no good with computers.	.49*	0.000
54	I am sure I could learn a computer language.	.48*	0.000
84	I need a firm mastery of computers for my work.	.84*	0.000
88	Anything that a computer can be used for I can do just as well some other way.	.31*	0.000
92	People who don't know how to use a computer cannot function in modern society.	.26*	0.000
99	Computers service little use in my life.	.49*	0.000

Note. *Correlation is significant at the 0.01 level (two tailed).

The second tactic used to support the construct validity of the Regan CCABS is

through comparison of purposive subjects and their scores on the three subscales of the

instrument. A subset of participants (n = 25 or 17.4% of all participants) was identified

as having high computer skills based upon their vocational positions (computer professionals and technical trainers) or their self-reported ranking on the CCABS

(Yacovelli, 2004) as described in chapter 3.

Subjects were then asked to rate themselves on the other two phenomena

(attitudes toward computers and attitude toward e-learning) using the CCABS (Yacovelli,

2004). The three questions on the CCABS directly relate to the three sections of the

Regan CCABS. The mean score on this instrument's first scale, which was "On a scale of

1 to 10, I rate my ability to use a computer (or computer skills) as . . .," was 7.76 for these

"experts" ($SD = 0.88$).

Mean scores of Question 1 (computer skills) of the CCABS (Yacovelli, 2004) and

Section 3: Self-Reported Computer Competence of the Regan CCABS for the subset of

subjects ($n = 25$) achieved a correlation coefficient of 0.63 ($p < 0.001$). Question 2

(attitudes toward computers) of the CCABS and Section 4: Attitudes Toward Computers

of the Regan CCABS achieved a correlation coefficient of 0.63 ($p < 0.001$) for these

same subjects. Question 3 (attitudes toward e-learning) of the CCABS and Section 5:

Attitudes Toward e-Learning of the Regan CCABS achieved a correlation coefficient of

0.62 ($p < 0.001$) for these subjects. Table 10 summarizes the findings from this particular

set of analysis regarding the construct validity of the Regan CCABS.

To gather data to help support the instrument's criterion-related validity, the

author conducted a correlation analysis of questions used in the Regan CCABS that were

garnered from existing instruments to those that were newly created for use within the

instrument. The author also compared these to the overall total of the subsection as well

for each of the three sections of the Regan CCABS instrument.

For Section 3: Self-Reported Computer Competence, this analysis entailed the

correlation coefficients of the Computer Attitude and Experience Scale (Potosky &

Bobko, 1998), which are Questions 12-19, 25, 29, 33, and 34 in the newly developed

Regan CCABS, the questions garnered from the unnamed instrument by Koroghlanian

and Brinkerhoff (2000), which are Questions 35-47 of the Regan CCABS; and the

questions originally developed for the Regan CCABS (Questions 11, 20-28, 30-32, and

48-50). These were also compared to the overall score of Section 3 of the Regan CCABS.

Overall, the newly created questions of the Regan CCABS correlated significantly with

both existing instruments.

Table 10

Correlations Between CCABS and Regan CCABS Subtotals

		Regan CCABS section		
CCABS question		Self-reported computer competence	Attitudes toward computers	Attitudes toward e-learning
Computer skills	Pearson correlation	.630*		
	Sig. (2-tailed)	.001		
	N	25		
Attitudes toward computers	Pearson correlation		.630*	
	Sig. (2-tailed)		.001	
	N		25	
Attitudes toward e-learning	Pearson correlation			.620*
	Sig. (2-tailed)			.001
	N			25

Note. CCABS = Computer Competence, Attitude, and Behavior Survey (Yacovelli, 2004); Regan CCABS from Yacovelli (2004b). *Correlation is significant at the 0.01 level (2-tailed).

The Regan CCABS original questions achieved a correlation coefficient of 0.71 with the questions from the CUES (Potosky & Bobko, 1998), and the correlation coefficient of 0.77 was achieved between these newly created questions and those questions from the unnamed instrument by Koroghlanian and Brinkerhoff. In addition, the newly created questions from the Regan CCABS correlated significantly with the overall subtotal of the section, achieving a correlation coefficient of a significant 0.91. This was slightly higher than those achieved from the CUES questions (0.89) but slightly less than those achieved by Koroghlanian and Brinkerhoff's questions (0.94). All correlations in Section 3 were significant at the 0.01 level. Table 11 displays the correlation coefficients achieved between the various questions comprised of Section 3 of the Regan CCABS and the overall subtotal achieved in this research study.

For Sections 4: Attitudes Toward Computers, the author analyzed the correlation coefficients of the CAS (Loyd & Gressard, 1984), which were Questions 51-90 of the Regan CCABS; the questions originally created for this study (Questions 91-100); and the overall subscore of this section of the instrument. The questions written for this research study achieved a correlation coefficient of 0.82 with the questions from the CAS (Loyd & Gressard, 1984), significant at the 0.01 level. These original questions also correlated significantly with the overall subtotal of the section, achieving a correlation coefficient of 0.88 (also significant at the 0.01 level). Comparatively, the CAS questions achieved a correlation coefficient of 0.99 to the overall subtotal of this section of the Regan CCABS (significant at the 0.01 level). Table 12 summarizes the correlation coefficients achieved between the various questions comprised of Section 4 of the Regan CCABS and the overall subtotal achieved in this research study.

Table 11

Correlations Between Questions on the Regan CCABS Section 3, Self-Reported Computer Competence, and CUES, UI, Regan CCABS New Questions, and Regan CCABS Overall

Self-reported computer competence and	Statistics	Self-reported computer competence and			
		CUES[1]	UI[1]	New questions	Overall subtotal for all questions
CUES	Pearson correlation		.770*	.710*	.890*
	Sig. (2-tailed)		.000	.000	.000
	N		144	144	144
UI	Pearson correlation	.770*		.770*	.940
	Sig. (2-tailed)	.000		.000	.000
	N	144		144	144
Regan CCABS new questions	Pearson correlation	.710*	.710*		.910*
	Sig. (2-tailed)	.000	.000		.000
	N	144	144		144
Regan CCABS all questions	Pearson correlation	.890*	.400*	.910*	
	Sig. (2 –tailed)	.000	.000	.000	
	N	144	144	144	

Note. CCABS = Computer Competence, Attitude, and Behavior Survey; CUES = Computer Understanding and Experience Scale (Potosky & Bobko, 1998); UI = unnamed instrument (Koroghlanian & Brinkerhoff, 2000). *Correlation is significant at the 0.01 level (2-tailed). [1]Not all questions from the CUES and UI were used.

Finally, for Section 5: Attitudes Toward e-Learning, the author analyzed the correlation coefficients of the unnamed instrument by Koroghlanian and Brinkerhoff (2000), which are Questions 101-118 of the Regan CCABS; the questions originally created for this study (Questions 119-130); and the overall subscore of this section of the instrument. The Regan original questions achieved a correlation coefficient of 0.91 with

the questions from Koroghlanian and Brinkerhoff's unnamed instrument, significant at

the 0.01 level. These original questions also correlated significantly with the overall

subtotal of the section, achieving a correlation coefficient of 0.97 (also significant at the

0.01 level).

Table 12

Correlations Between Questions on the Regan CCABS Section 4, Attitudes Toward Computers, and CAS, Regan CCABS New Questions, and Regan CCABS Overall

| Attitudes toward computers and | Statistics | Attitudes toward computers and | | |
		CAS[1]	New questions	Overall subtotal for all questions
CAS	Pearson correlation		.820*	.990*
	Sig. (2-tailed)		.000	.000
	N		144	144
Regan CCABS new questions	Pearson correlation	.810*		.880*
	Sig. (2-tailed)	.000		.000
	N	144		144
Regan CCABS all questions	Pearson correlation	.990*	.880*	
	Sig. (2 –tailed)	.000	.000	
	N	144	144	

Note. CCABS = Computer Competence, Attitude, and Behavior Survey; CAS = Computer Attitudes Scales (Loyd & Gressard, 1984). *Correlation is significant at the 0.01 level (2-tailed). [1]Not all questions from the CAS were used.

Comparatively, the questions from Koroghlanian and Brinkerhoff's (2000)

unnamed instrument achieved a correlation coefficient of 0.98 to the overall subtotal of this section of the Regan CCABS (significant at the 0.01 level). Table 13 summarizes the

correlation coefficients achieved between the various questions comprised of Section 5 of

the Regan CCABS and the overall subtotal achieved in this research study.

Table 13

Correlations Between Questions on the Regan CCABS Section 5, Attitudes Toward e-Learning, and UI,
Regan CCABS New Questions, and Regan CCABS Overall

Attitudes toward computers and	Statistics	Attitudes toward computers and		
		UI[1]	New questions	Overall subtotal for all questions
UI	Pearson correlation		.910*	.980*
	Sig. (2-tailed)		.000	.000
	N		144	144
Regan CCABS new questions	Pearson correlation	.920*		.970*
	Sig. (2-tailed)	.000		.000
	N	144		144
Regan CCABS all questions	Pearson correlation	.980*	.971*	
	Sig. (2 –tailed)	.000	.000	
	N	144	144	

Note. CCABS = Computer Competence, Attitude, and Behavior Survey; UI = unnamed instrument
(Koroghlanian & Brinkerhoff, 2000). *Correlation is significant at the 0.01 level (2-tailed). [1]Not all
questions from the UI were used.

In summary, the validity analysis for the Regan CCABS consisted of efforts to

support the four types of validity: face, content, construct, and criterion related

(American Psychological Association, 1985; Ravid, 2000). These included the analysis of

four subject-matter experts (face and content validity), an analysis of the three measured subscales' scores and their correlation between each of the individual items comprising the three subsections (construct validity), a comparison of purposive subjects and their scores on the three subscales of the instrument (construct validity), and an analysis of questions used in the Regan CCABS that were garnered from existing instruments and their correlation to the questions that were newly created for use within the instrument (criterion-related validity).

Reliability analysis of the *Regan CCABS.* Two different tactics were used to gather data to support the instrument's overall reliability. First, the author conducted a test-retest scenario on a sample of those who participated in the overall study. Then the instrument was readministered to the sample ($n = 7$) at least 7 days after submitting their original survey. In Section 3: Self-Reported Computer Competence (a.k.a. "What Do You Know about Computers?"), a Pearson correlation coefficient of 0.82 was achieved (significant at the 0.05 level). Section 4: Attitudes Toward Computers (a.k.a. "What Do You Think About Computers?") resulted in a Pearson correlation coefficient of 0.92, and Section 5: Attitudes Toward e-Learning (a.k.a. "What Do You Think About Internet-Delivered Training?") resulted in a correlation coefficient of 0.97 (both significant at the 0.01 level). These findings are represented in Table 14.

The second area of analysis to help establish the instrument's reliability was using the split-half technique. The three subscales of the Regan CCABS were equally divided (even questions to odd questions), yielding a total of six subscales (two for each phenomenon being investigated). The two subscales for each phenomenon were then correlated to see if a correlation exists between the two halves.

For Section 3: Self-Reported Computer Competence (a.k.a. "What Do You Know about Computers?"), the two scores from the split subsection (odd Questions 11-40 and even Questions 10-50, respectively) achieved a correlation coefficient of 0.93, a

significant correlation at the 0.01 level. The two halves of Section 4: Attitudes Toward

Computers (a.k.a. "What Do You Think about Computers?") were divided into odd

(Questions 51-99) and even (Questions 52-100) halves, and these achieved a correlation

coefficient of 0.94 (also at the 0.01 level). The two halves of Section 5: Attitudes Toward

e-Learning (a.k.a. "What Do You Think about Internet-Delivered Training?") achieved a

correlation coefficient of 0.94 (at the 0.01 level). These results are displayed in Table 15.

Table 14

Test-Retest Correlations on the Regan CCABS

Attempt 1 Regan CCABS section		Attempt 2 Regan CCABS section		
		Self-reported computer competence	Attitudes toward computers	Attitudes toward e-learning
Self-reported computer competence	Pearson correlation	.820*		
	Sig. (2-tailed)	.024		
	N	7		
Attitudes toward computers	Pearson correlation		.920**	
	Sig. (2-tailed)		.004	
	N		7	
Attitudes toward e-learning	Pearson correlation			.970**
	Sig. (2-tailed)			.000
	N			7

Note. CCABS = Regan Computer Competence, Attitude, and Behavior Survey. *Correlation is significant at the 0.05 level (2-tailed). **Correlation is significant at the 0.01 level (2-tailed).

In summary, the reliability analysis for the Regan CCABS consisted of two analyses. First, a test-retest scenario was conducted on a sample of those who participated

in the overall study. Second, the author employed the split-half technique on all three

subscales of the Regan CCABS.

Table 15

Split-Half Correlations on the Regan CCABS

Split-half odd Regan CCABS questions	Statistics	Split-half even Regan CCABS questions		
		Self-reported computer competence (10-50)	Attitudes toward computers (52-100)	Attitudes toward e-learning (102-130)
Self-reported computer competence (11-49)	Pearson correlation	.930*		
	Sig. (2-tailed)	.000		
	N	144		
Attitudes toward computers (51-99)	Pearson correlation		.940*	
	Sig. (2-tailed)		.000	
	N		144	
Attitudes toward e-learning (101-129)	Pearson correlation			.940*
	Sig. (2-tailed)			.000
	N			144

Note. CCABS = Computer Competence, Attitude, and Behavior Survey. *Correlation is significant at the 0.01 level (2-tailed).

Hypotheses Testing

In addition to the validity and reliability analyses, the author examined certain hypotheses in this research study to either support or refute claims made in previous studies, as noted in chapter 2. The following hypotheses were tested:

1. Subjects' attitudes toward computers will be positively correlated with their attitude toward e-learning as a method of learning. This hypothesis was tested using the data gathered from Section 4: Attitudes Toward Computers and Section 5: Attitudes Toward Internet-Delivered Training of the Regan CCABS. Attitudes toward computers were positively correlated with attitudes toward e-learning as noted by the achievement of a correlation coefficient of 0.72 between the two mean subscores of these sections (significant at the 0.01 level). Therefore, the null hypothesis can be rejected.

2. Subjects' age is negatively correlated with self-reported computer competence. This hypothesis was tested using the demographic data gathered from Section 1: Participant Demographics and mean subscore from Section 3: Self-Reported Computer Competence of the Regan CCABS. Using a one-way ANOVA procedure, the difference among the means was statistically significant at the 0.03 level ($F = 2.29$, $df = 8,135$). The Levene test for homogeneity of variances obtained a significance value of 0.25, suggesting that the variances for the age groups are equal and the assumption that the variances of the groups are all equal is justified. Although age is negatively correlated with overall self-reported computer competence, the relationship is very weak (correlation coefficient of -0.27, significant at the 0.01 level). Therefore, the author rejects the null hypothesis ($p < 0.01$).

3. Subjects' age is negatively correlated with attitudes toward e-learning. This hypothesis was tested using the demographic data gathered from Section 1: Participant Demographics and mean subscores of Section 5: Attitudes Toward Internet-Delivered Training of the Regan CCABS. The data suggest that age are not significantly correlated

to attitudes toward e-learning (correlation coefficient of 0.14 achieved where $p < 0.10$). Based upon these data, the author accepts the null hypothesis.

4. The author examined if subjects' level of education is positively correlated with their attitudes toward e-learning. Like Hypothesis 3, this hypothesis was tested using data gathered from Section 1: Participant Demographics and 5: Attitudes Toward Internet-Delivered Training of the Regan CCABS. Educational attainment is not significantly correlated to attitudes toward e-learning (correlation coefficient of -0.16 achieved, where $p < 0.05$). Based upon these data, the author determined that this hypothesis is not statistically significant.

5. Subjects' self-reported computer competence was positively correlated with overall attitudes toward e-learning. This hypothesis was tested using the data gathered from Section 3: Self-Reported Computer Competence and Section and 5: Attitudes Toward Internet-Delivered Training of the Regan CCABS. It was determined that attitudes toward computers are positively correlated with attitudes toward e-learning (correlation coefficient of 0.52, significant at the 0.001 level). Therefore, the author rejects the null hypothesis.

6. There was no significant difference between gender and attitudes toward computers, attitudes toward technology-enabled learning, and self-reported computer competence. Using an independent samples t test, this hypothesis was tested using the demographic data gathered from Section 1: Participant Demographics and the subscores from the three subscales of the Regan CCABS. Although no significant difference was found between the means of gender with regard to Section 4: Attitudes Toward Computers and Section 5: Attitudes Toward e-Learning, a significant difference was discovered between the means of males and females with regard to Section 3: Self-

Reported Computer Competence. According to the data, males have a slightly higher

self-reported computer competence score ($M = 4.22$, $SD = 0.54$) than females ($M = 3.88$,

$SD = 0.64$). Therefore, the author determined that there was a significant correlation

between gender and self-reported computer competence, a significant correlation between

gender and attitudes toward both computer and e-learning to be statistically significant.

Table 16 displays the data regarding gender and the subscores for the Regan CCABS.

Table 16

Correlations Between Gender and the Three Subscales of the Regan CCABS

								95% confidence interval of difference	
Regan CCABS					*t* test for equality of means				
					Sig. (2-	Mean	*SE*		
section subscore	F	Sig.	*t*	*df*	tailed)	difference	difference	Lower	Upper
Self-reported computer competence	1.15	0.20	3.30	142	0.001	0.33	0.10	0.13	0.53
Attitudes toward computers	0.34	0.56	0.67	142	0.502	0.06	0.09	-0.11	0.23
Attitudes toward e-learning	1.27	0.26	0.42	142	0.672	-0.04	0.10	0.25	0.16

Note. CCABS = Computer Competence, Attitude, and Behavior Survey; equal variances assumed for Levene's Test for Equality of Variances.

Chapter Summary

In summary, this research study focused on the development of a valid and

reliable instrument to measure three phenomena: subjects' attitudes toward computers,

their attitudes toward e-learning, and their self-reported computer competence. This

chapter describes the results of the implementation of the research described in chapter 3, including the types of statistical analysis used to help establish the instrument's validity and reliability.

One-hundred-forty-four subjects participated in the research study over a 2-week period. Participants received a paper version of the Regan CCABS where the higher the score, the more positive the attitudes toward computers and e-learning and the higher the self-reported computer competence. All participants were over the age of 18; the largest group (43%) was between the ages of 30 and 39. The population was closely split between males and females. Although the minority of participants ($N = 54$) completed the paper version of the instrument, the majority ($N = 90$) chose to complete the survey via the Internet. Over half the participants reported having taken an Internet-delivered course, and almost all reported owning a computer. Participants' overall self-reported computer competence was relatively high ($M = 4.03$ out of 5.00), and their overall attitudes toward computers were relatively positive ($M = 4.25$ out of 5.00).

The author followed several procedures to gather data to support the four types of validity (American Psychological Association, 1985; Leedy, 2001; Ravid, 2000). Face validity analysis was conducted by the author as well as select subject-matter experts familiar with educational evaluation and measurement and the three phenomena being examined in the instrument. The instrument's content validity was examined by these same subject-matter experts, who analyzed the instrument to ensure it analyzed the three phenomena (self-reported computer competence, attitudes toward computers, and attitudes toward e-learning). They provided feedback on each item as it related to the subscales, and all subject-matter experts agreed that the instrument did specifically explore the three phenomena in question.

Two strategies were employed to collect data to support the instrument's overall construct validity: (a) analysis of the overall correlations between the scores of each of the three measured subscales of the instrument and their correlation between each of the individual items comprising the three subsections and (b) using a subsample of the overall population ($n = 25$), overall subscores were correlated with results of a second instrument, the CCABS (Yacovelli, 2004). Both tactics yielded significant correlations to support the over construct validity of the instrument.

Finally, for criterion-related validity, the author performed a correlation analysis of questions used in the Regan CCABS that were garnered from existing instruments to those that were newly created for use within the instrument. The author also compared these to the overall total of the subsection as well for each of the three sections of the Regan CCABS. Correlations between all variables were found to be significant ($p <$ 0.01), further supporting the overall validity of the newly developed instrument.

Two tactics were employed to help establish the instrument's reliability: (a) a test-retest scenario on a subsample of those who participated in the overall study ($N = 7$) and (b) the split-half technique. Both tactics yielded significant correlations to support the reliability of the Regan CCABS.

Hypotheses were also tested in this research study to either support or refute claims made in previous studies. Of the six hypotheses analyzed, four were determined to be statistically significant: (a) subjects' overall attitudes toward computers were positively correlated with attitudes toward e-learning (Hypothesis 1), (b) age was found to be a statistically significant variable on self-reported computer competence (Hypothesis 2), (c) subjects' self-reported computer competence was positively correlated with overall attitudes toward e-learning (Hypothesis 5), and (d) data suggest gender is significantly correlated with self-reported computer competence with males in the group reporting slightly higher computer competence scores than females in the study (a facet of Hypothesis 6). The remaining hypotheses were not found to be statistically significant: (a) age was not found to affect attitudes toward e-learning (Hypothesis 3), (b) education levels were not found to be correlated with attitudes toward e-learning (Hypothesis 4), and (c) gender was not found to be significant in relationship to attitudes toward computers or attitudes toward technology-enabled learning (a facet of Hypothesis 6).

Chapter 5: Discussion

Introduction

The corporate sector is quickly embracing e-learning and technology-enabled learning to accomplish many of its training and learning objectives. However, many corporations are delving into technology-enabled learning without understanding their end user's computer competence or attitude; they are simply launching e-learning efforts without determining if an e-learning solution is right for a particular business environment from a learner's perspective. Although there are several instruments that measure attitudes toward computers and self-reported computer competence, most are designed to assess American college undergraduates and K-12 learners, and they may not have applicability to the corporate, adult learners in the early 21st century. Few instruments exist that are applicable to the corporate adult learner that specifically address attitudes toward technology-enabled learning or e-learning.

This research study focused on the development of a valid and reliable instrument to measure subjects' attitudes toward computers, attitudes toward e-learning, and self-reported computer competence. The newly developed instrument, named the Regan CCABS, consists of five sections: (a) Participant Demographics, (b) Organization Demographics, (c) Self-Reported Computer Competence, (d) Attitudes Toward Computers, and (e) Attitudes Toward Internet-Delivered Training (totaling 130 items). Each section was comprised of entirely new questions for this research or a combination of existing instruments whose validity and reliability have been explored extensively in previous studies and newly created questions by the author. Each section is scored so that higher scores are indicative of more positive attitudes or higher perceived computer competence. Participants had the option to complete the instrument via paper or the

Internet.

In addition to the reliability and validity analysis, hypotheses were examined in this research study. Various authors hypothesized about the correlation between certain variables (such as gender and attitude toward computers), and this study looked at six such hypotheses to either support or refute claims made in previous studies or to briefly analyze these types of relationships for the first time.

A total of 144 subjects participated in the study, which was comprised of both purposive sampling (in conjunction with the validity testing of the newly created instrument) and convenience sampling for the initial distribution of the instrument. Subjects met two simple criteria: (a) were at least 18 years of age (thus constituted as adults) and (b) worked within a corporate or not-for profit organization that is nonacademic (meaning not K-12 or higher education environments). A small subsample of subjects met the additional criteria of ranking themselves has having high or low self-reported computer competence on a secondary instrument, and these variables were later used in the validity and reliability analysis (as noted in chapter 4). Subjects were from a variety of vocational settings, including a large national insurance company, a regional law firm, and a local municipal government agency.

Discussion of Results

Instrument validity. According to the *Standards for Educational and Psychological Testing* (American Psychological Association, 1985), there are three types of validity: content validity, criterion-related validity, and construct validity. A fourth type of validity, face validity was also mentioned by several authors as a means of helping to establish the overall validity for an instrument (Leedy & Ormrod, 2001; Ravid, 2000). The data were analyzed in order to determine if the instrument was a valid

instrument in all four facets of validity (American Psychological Association; Leedy &
Ormrod; Ravid).

Face validity refers to the degree to which the instrument appears to measure the
intended phenomenon (Leedy & Ormrod, 2001; Ravid, 2000). Face validity for the
Regan CCABS was established by the author as well as select subject-matter experts
familiar with educational evaluation and measurement and the three phenomena being
examined in the instrument.

Content validity is the degree to which an instrument is a representative sample of
the content area (or domain) being measured (American Psychological Association,
1985; Leedy & Ormrod, 2001; Ravid, 2000). The instrument's content validity was also
confirmed by the same group of subject-matter experts. The subject-matter experts
analyzed the instrument to ensure it analyzed the three phenomena (self-reported
computer competence, attitudes toward computers, and attitudes toward e-learning). They
provided feedback on each item as it related to the subscales, and all subject-matter
experts agreed that the instrument did specifically explore the three phenomena in
question.

Construct validity refers to the extent to which an instrument measures and
provides accurate information about a theoretical trait or characteristic (American
Psychological Association, 1985; Leedy & Ormrod, 2001; Ravid, 2000). Two strategies
were employed to collect data to support the instrument's overall construct validity: (a)
analysis of the overall correlations between the scores of each of the three measured
subscales of the instrument and their correlation between each of the individual items
comprising the three subsections and (b) using a subsample of the overall population ($n =$
25), overall subscores were correlated with results of a second instrument, the CCABS

(Yacovelli, 2004). Both tactics revealed data to support the over construct validity of the instrument.

Criterion-related validity refers to the extent to which the performance of an instrument of measurement correlates with another well-established instrument, which purports to measure the same phenomenon (American Psychological Association, 1985; Leedy & Ormrod, 2001; Ravid, 2000). Data to support the criterion-related validity were found within all three sections of the Regan CCABS. Newly created items in Section 3 significantly correlated with pre-existing items: the CUES by Potosky and Bobko (1998) and the unnamed instrument by Koroghlanian and Brinkerhoff (2000). The newly developed questions from Section 4 were also found to correlate significantly with the questions from Loyd and Gressard's (1984) CAS, and a significant correlation coefficient between all questions and the CAS was also achieved. The questions newly developed by the author for Section 5 significantly correlated with the questions from Koroghlanian and Brinkerhoff's unnamed instrument; an overall subtotal correlation coefficient was also discovered.

Instrument reliability. This research study focused on the development of a valid and reliable instrument to measure subjects' attitudes toward computers, attitudes toward e-learning, and self-reported computer competence. The data suggest that the Regan CCABS is indeed a reliable instrument. Two tactics were used to support the overall reliability of the Regan CCABS: (a) a test-retest scenario on a sample of those who participated in the overall study and (b) a split-half technique.

The author conducted a test-retest analysis in an effort to gather data to establish the validity of the Regan CCABS. The instrument was readministered to the sample ($n =$ 7) at least 7 days after submitting their original survey. All three sections (Section 3: Self-

Reported Computer Competence, Section 4: Attitudes Toward Computers, and Section 5:

Attitudes Toward e-Learning) achieved Pearson correlation coefficients of 0.82, 0.92, and

0.97, respectively. Gable (1986) commented that reliability figures of above 0.70 are

acceptable levels for an attitude measure.

The author also conducted a split-half analysis in a further attempt to gather data

to establish the validity of the Regan CCABS. The three subscales of the Regan CCABS

were equally divided (even questions to odd questions), yielding a total of six subscales

(two for each phenomenon being investigated). The two subscales for each phenomenon

were then analyzed to see if a correlation exists between the two halves. The two halves

of Section 3: Self-Reported Computer Competence achieved a correlation coefficient of

0.93 ($p < 0.01$). Section 4: Attitudes Toward Computers achieved a correlation

coefficient of 0.94 ($p < 0.01$). Finally, Section 5: Attitudes Toward e-Learning achieved a

correlation coefficient of 0.94 ($p < 0.01$). Again, all three sections achieved acceptable

levels of reliability.

Hypotheses analysis. Hypotheses were also examined in this research study. The

author found significant results in four of the six hypotheses analyzed. All hypotheses are

described in detail below:

1. It was found that subjects' overall attitudes toward computers were positively

correlated with attitudes toward e-learning. This hypothesis was tested using the means

gathered from Section 4: Attitudes Toward Computers and Section 5: Attitudes Toward

Internet-Delivered Training of the Regan CCABS. Although no previous studies were

identified to either support or refute these conclusions, this author believes these two

phenomena correlate due to participants' comfort level with technology--be that with

computers in general or when they are specifically used for learning. In other words, this author believes those subjects who are more at ease with technology will have more positive attitudes toward using technology for learning.

2. The author hypothesized that subjects' age would negatively correlate with self-reported computer competence. This hypothesis was tested using the demographic data gathered from Section 1 and mean subscores from Section 3: Self-Reported Computer Competence of the Regan CCABS. Using a one-way ANOVA procedure, the difference among the means was statistically significant at the 0.03 level. The Levene test for homogeneity of variances obtained a significance value of 0.25, suggesting that the variances for the age groups are equal and the assumption that the variances of the groups are all equal is justified. Although age did negatively correlate with overall self-reported computer competence significantly, it should be noted that the relationship is very weak (correlation coefficient of -0.27, significant at the 0.01 level), which is similar to findings made by Koohang (1986) and Pope-Davis and Twig (1991). Although a weak significant correlation does exist between age and self-reported computer competence, this author believes that other variables, such as computer experience, have a more significant impact on self-reported computer competence than age with this particular population. Further analysis needs to be conducted in order to ascertain if age truly is a factor with regard to self-reported computer competence.

3. In this research study, age was not found to relate to attitudes toward e-learning. This hypothesis was tested using the demographic data gathered from Section 1: Participant Demographics and mean subscores of Section 5: Attitudes Toward Internet-Delivered Training of the Regan CCABS. These results are similar to the conclusions obtained by Sanders and Morrison-Shetlar (2001). Like the findings of this research study in relationship to age and self-reported computer competence, this author believes that

age does not affect attitudes toward e-learning because other variables, such as computer experience, have a more significant impact on attitudes toward e-learning than age.

4. In this research study, education levels were not found to correlate significantly with attitudes toward e-learning, which was also a finding reported by Sanders and Morrison-Shetlar (2001). This hypothesis was tested using data gathered from Section 1: Participant Demographics and Section 5: Attitudes Toward Internet-Delivered Training of the Regan CCABS. Based upon these findings, the author concludes that age and educational attainment levels do not affect attitudes toward e-learning because other variables, such as computer experience, have a more significant impact on attitudes toward e-learning than age.

5. In this research study, subjects' self-reported computer competence was positively correlated with overall attitudes toward e-learning. Similar to Hypothesis 1, no previous studies were identified that either support or refute these conclusions. This author believes these findings occurred due to participants being more comfortable with the technology and, therefore, less apprehensive toward computers or e-learning. In other words, the more computer-savvy the participant, the more positive they are with using computers for learning.

6. This author examined gender in relationship to the three phenomena measured by the Regan CCABS with this hypothesis. Similar to the findings by Anderson et al. (1980) and Murphy et al. (1988), data suggest gender is significantly correlated with self-reported computer competence (Section 3) with males in the group reporting slightly higher computer competence scores than females. However, this is contrary to the findings by Woodrow (1992, 1994), who either did not find significant differences in gender and self-reported computer competence or found that females possessed

significantly higher self-reported computer competence than males. Because of these discrepancies, the author concludes that further analysis needs to be conducted in order to ascertain if gender truly is a factor with regard to self-reported computer competence.

In addition, this study found that no significant relationship exists between gender and attitudes toward computers on Section 4 of the Regan CCABS or gender and attitudes toward technology-enabled learning on Section 5 of the Regan CCASB. These findings are similar to those of Koohang (1989), Koroghlanian and Brinkerhoff (2000), Pope-Davis and Twig (1991), and Woodrow (1992, 1994), but they are contradictory to the findings of Kay (1993a, 1993b), Koohang (1986), Loyd and Gressard (1986), Raub (1981), Sanders and Morrison-Shetlar (2001), and Smith and Necessary (1996). Although this author hypothesizes that experience actually has a more significant impact than gender in relationship to learner attitudes toward computers or e-learning, it is recommended that more research be done in the realm of gender and attitudes toward computers and attitudes toward e-learning.

Implications

Although it has been shown that e-learning and training delivered via the Internet and other technologies offers a myriad of financial benefits to an organization (Rosenberg, 2001; Rossett, 2002; Urban & Weggen, 2000), this type of training delivery method will not succeed if the end users of this training do not believe they have the skills to use it (Bandura, 1977, 1986; Schunk, 1984), have negative attitudes toward technology (Bear, 1990; Loyd & Gressard, 1984; Murphy et al., 1988), or have negative attitudes toward e-learning (Coll Garcia, 2001; Koroghlanian & Brinkerhoff, 2000; Sanders & Morrison-Shetlar, 2001). Reece and Gable (1982) noted the use of computers for learning "could be a waste of time and money if proper curricula and laboratory experiences do not support the development of positive attitudes toward using these machines to facilitate learning" (p. 913).

Prior to implementing any e-learning strategy, corporate leaders can now benchmark their employees on the three phenomena: attitudes toward computers, attitudes toward e-learning, and self-reported computer competence as measured in the Regan CCABS. As noted earlier in the literature, studies show that an individual's self-reported computer competence is a critical predictor for the use of computer technology (Delcourt & Kinzie, 1993; Jorde-Bloom, 1988; Kinzie et al., 1994). In addition, the literature has also shown that understanding employees' attitudes toward these phenomena is important for the successful adoption of technology (Davis et al., 1989; Zoltan & Chapanis, 1982) as several studies have looked at how negative attitudes toward computers can influence the learning process, and student's attitudes can enhance or hinder knowledge acquisition (e.g., Griswold, 1983; Koohang, 1987, 1989; Marcoulides, 1989, 1991). Without a high level of computer competence or positive attitudes toward the technology, the benefits that e-learning has within the corporate sector regarding cost-effectiveness, access to learning modules both synchronously and asynchronously, and more effective use of training resources and, therefore, higher return on investment of certain training expenditures could be in jeopardy (Rosenberg, 2001; Rossett, 2002; Urban & Weggen, 2000). Therefore, e-learning is of high value not only for the educational advantages it provides but also for its fiscal benefits to the company as well as noted above. If after analyzing the data, corporate leaders determine that employees need to increase their level of computer competence or need to increase their overall attitudes toward computer or e-learning, intervention efforts can be focused at the desired area to prepare the learners to be the most successful when it comes to the implementation and use of technology-enabled learning solutions for employee training and development.

Conversely, if an e-learning strategy has already been implemented at a particular corporation and challenges have surfaced with regard to employees' satisfaction with training delivery, then the training and development leadership could utilize this instrument to ascertain learners' attitudes toward computers, attitudes toward e-learning, and self-reported computer competence. These data would help ascertain if the challenges associated with the e-learning's effectiveness are due to the learners' personal barriers toward this type of training delivery or if perhaps the challenge is due to other factors, such as poor instructional design practices. Again, the instrument can help identify the areas of improvement for the e-learning delivery.

Recommendations

Although this research has provided some insight into the three phenomena of attitudes toward computers, attitudes toward e-learning, and self-reported computer competence and the corporate, adult learner, there are several areas of opportunity for further research. First, because data have been garnered to support the overall validity and reliability of the current version of the Regan CCABS, it is recommended that the number of items in the instrument be reduced and yet still yield the same reliability and validity. Specifically, it is suggested that those items whose Item-to-Subtotal correlation was below 0.51 (Questions 16, 18, 30, 32, 33, 52, 53, 54, 84, 88, 92, 99, and 106) would immediately be eliminated to reduce the number of items and still retain the overall reliability and validity of the instrument. Reducing the number of items will help create a shorter survey with the same level of validity and reliability, and reduce the risk of rater dropout where participants fail to complete the instrument due to lost interest with a longer form (Tull & Albaum, 1973). Once the next version of the Regan CCABS is created, data to retest its reliability and validity should be garnered, using the same processes performed by this author as detailed in chapter 3.

Second, it is recommended that a replication study be done to broaden the population of the original study. Although data from the Regan CCABS has been found to support the overall validity and reliability of the instrument, it is recommended that the variety of subjects be expanded to include a wider range of ages, vocational settings, and comfort with computers. In addition, 68% of participants ($n = 98$) identified themselves as being salaried workers (while 27% classified themselves as hourly). It is recommended that more hourly employees be included in samples for future studies.. The broader subject base will help to further confirm or reject the trends identified in the hypothesis analyses both from this study and previous studies.

This study focused on the corporate, adult learner within the contemporary North American workplace. A third recommendation is to conduct comparative analyses of the findings from this study and those of college students and non-North American adult working professionals using the Regan CCABS. Does the college experience in today's contemporary climate help or hinder the three phenomena described? Do business professionals within non-North American cultures possess more positive attitudes toward computers and e-learning or less? Similar to the second recommendation, this would broaden the analysis to help determine if the trends associated with this study hold true with different populations.

Fourth, this study revealed many unsolicited comments from participants regarding their attitudes toward e-learning overall. During the data-collection phase of the research, the author received such comments as the following:

1. "Internet classes save employees time away from their workstations."

2. "I do not like internet [sic] training when it has to be done at my desk. It is very hard to concentrate due to the noise level in the office and other distractions."

3. "I can set my own pace and not be distracted by other students who aren't interested in learning or want to demonstrate how smart they think they are."

4. "I am comfortable doing a survey online. I am not, however, excited about e-learning. I understand that it is oftentimes a more efficient delivery system for learning, but it is seldom done well and I have implemented CBT courses only when I have to ." These comments provide insight into the participants' attitudes that is not as easily revealed within a quantitative research approach. Therefore, it is recommended that a qualitative study commence regarding adults' attitudes toward e-learning to see if similar themes are uncovered in a qualitative study similar to those discovered in this quantitative study.

This study found that subjects' overall attitudes toward computers were positively correlated with attitudes toward e-learning (Hypothesis 1), and subjects' self-reported computer competence was positively correlated with overall attitudes toward e-learning (Hypothesis 5). Therefore, because no previous studies were found to support or refute these findings, a fifth recommendation is to examine the correlation between attitudes toward e-learning and attitudes toward computers overall and self-reported computer competence. It is important to understand these relationships further, and explore these relationships on a larger population to determine if the findings from this study are trends or merely unique to the sample of this study.

The literature noted that, with regard to attitudes toward computers, experience is positively correlated toward attitude (i.e., Bear et al., 1987; Griswold, 1983; Loyd &

Gressard, 1984, 1986; Milbrath & Kinzie, 2000; Miller & Varma, 1993; Raub, 1981 Woodrow, 1992, 1994). Therefore, a final recommendation for future research is to examine the impact on previous experience with e-learning and how it has affected attitudes toward e-learning. Like the correlations found by numerous authors regarding experience with computers and their attitude toward them, does previous exposure to e-learning impact overall attitudes toward e-learning? This is an important phenomena to examine as e-learning becomes more and more prevalent within the modern workplace, but instructional design strategies vary greatly from one organization to the next.

The phenomena of attitudes toward computers, attitudes toward e-learning, and self-reported computer competence are important aspects to understand in our modern workplace. It is the hope of the author that this research will help training and development leaders ascertain the organizations' readiness for e-learning and truly examine their learners' preparedness to this form of training delivery to ensure that its implementation is as effective and satisfactory as possible for the organization's health; for the fiscal bottom line, and most importantly, for the corporate, adult learner.

References

Ajzen, I. (1988). *Attitudes, personality, and behavior*. Chicago: Dorsey Press.

American Management Association. (2003). The pay-offs of e-learning go far beyond the financial. *HR Focus, 80*(10), 7, 10.

American Psychological Association. (1985). *Standards for educational and psychological testing*. Washington, DC: Author.

Anderson, R. E. (1987). Females surpass males in computer problem solving: Findings from the Minnesota Computer Literacy Assessment. *Journal of Educational Computing Research, 3*(1), 39-51.

Anderson, R. E., & Klassen, D. L. (1981). A conceptual framework for developing computer literacy instruction. *Association for Educational Data Systems Journal, 14*, 128-150.

Anderson, R. E., Krohn, K., & Sandman, R. S. (1980). The Minnesota Literacy and Awareness Assessment Test. St. Paul: Minnesota Educational Computing Consortium.

Bandalos, D., & Benson, J. (1990). Testing the factor structure invariance of a computer attitude scale over two grouping conditions. *Educational and Psychological Measurement, 50*, 49-60.

Bandura, A. (1977). Self-efficacy: Toward a unifying theory of behavioral change. *Psychological Review, 84*, 191-215.

Bear, G. G. (1990). Knowledge of computer ethics: Its relationship to computer attitude and sociomoral reasoning. *Journal of Educational Computing Research, 6*, 77-87.

Bear, G. G., Richards, H., & Lancaster, P. (1987). Attitudes toward computers: Validation of a Computer Attitudes Scale. *Journal of Educational Computing Research, 3*, 207-218.

Bitter, G. G., & Davis, S. J. (1985). Measuring the development of computer literacy among teachers. *Association for Educational Data Systems Journal, 18*, 243-253.

Brennan, M. (2003). *Adoption, preference, and practice: A demand-side snapshot of e-learning content*. Framingham, MA: International Data Corporation.

Calvert, E. L. (1981). *A study of the relationship between level of mathematics anxiety and sex, age, mathematical background, and previous success in mathematics*. Unpublished manuscript, Western Illinois University, Macomb.

Chisholm, C. (1980). *Correlates of math avoidance responsible for filtering individuals from math/science areas*. Unpublished master's thesis, Towson State University, Towson, MD.

Christensen, R., & Knezek, G. (2000). Internal consistency reliabilities for 14 computer attitude scales. *Journal of Technology and Teacher Education, 8*, 327-336.

Clark, R. E. (2001). Media are "mere vehicles:" The opening argument. In R. E. Clark (Ed.), *Learning from media: Arguments, analysis, and evidence* (pp. 1-12). Greenwich, CT: Information Age Publishing.

Clark, R. E., & Sugrue, B. (2001). International views of the media debate. In R. E. Clark (Ed.), *Learning from media: Arguments, analysis, and evidence* (pp. 71-88). Greenwich, CT: Information Age Publishing.

Coggins, C. C. (1988). Preferred learning styles and their impact on completion of external degree programs. *The American Journal of Distance Education, 2*, 25-37.

Coll Garcia, J. F. (2001). An instrument to help teachers assess learners' attitudes towards multimedia instruction. *Education, 122*, 94-101.

Commission on Technology and Adult Learning. (2000, June). *A vision of e-learning for America's workforce*. Alexandria, VA: American Society for Training and Development and National Governors Association. Retrieved October 18, 2001, from http://www.astd.org/virtual_community/public_policy/jh_ver.pdf

Cronbach, L.J. & Snow, R.E. (1969). *Individual differences in learning ability as a function of instructional variables*. Stanford, CA: Stanford University, School of Education.

Davis, F. D., Bagozzi, R. P., & Warshaw, P. R. (1989). User acceptance of computer technology: A comparison of two theoretical models. *Management Science, 35*, 98-103.

Delcourt, M. A. B., & Kinzie, M. B. (1993). Computer technologies in teacher education: The measurement of attitudes and self-efficacy. *Journal of Research and Development in Education, 27*(1), 35-41.

Delcourt, M. A. B., & Lewis, L. (1987, February 19-20). *Measuring adults' attitudes toward computers: An initial investigation*. Paper presented at the Lifelong Learning Research Conference, College Park, MD.

Doll, W. J., & Torkzadeh, G. (1988). The measurement of end-user computing satisfaction. *MIS Quarterly, 12*, 259-274.

D'Souza, P. V. (1992). E-mail's role in the learning process: A case study. *Journal of Research on Computing in Education, 25*, 256-264.

Edwards, A. L. (1957). *Techniques of attitude scale construction*. New York: Appleton-Century-Crofts.

Erickson, T. E. (1987). Sex differences in student attitudes toward computers. *Journal of Educational Computing Research, 9*, 487-507.

Fennema, E. (1977). *Sex-related differences in mathematics achievement: Myths, realities, and related factors*. Washington, DC: National Institute of Education.

Fennema, E., & Sherman, J. A. (1976). Fennema-Sherman mathematics attitudes scales: Instruments designed to measure attitudes toward the learning of mathematics by females and males. *Journal of Research in Mathematics Education, 7*, 324-326.

Francis, L. J. (1993). Measuring attitude toward computers among undergraduate college students: The affective domain. *Computers in Education, 20*, 251-255.

Francis, L. J., & Evans, T. E. (1995). The reliability and validity of the Bath County Computer Attitude Scale. *Journal of Educational Computing Research, 12*, 135-146.

Gable, R. K. (1986). *Instrument development in the affective domain*. Boston: Kluwer-Nijhoff.

Gabriel, R. M. (1985). Assessing computer literacy: A validated instrument and empirical results. *Association for Educational Data Systems Journal, 18*, 153-171.

Gardner, D. G., Discenza, R., & Dukes, R. L. (1993). The measurement of computer attitudes: An empirical comparison of available scales. *Journal of Educational Computing Research, 9*, 487-507.

Gressard, C. P., & Loyd, B. H. (1985, March 31-April 4). *Validation studies of a new computer attitudes scale*. Paper presented at the annual meeting of the American Educational Research Association, Chicago.

Griswold, P. A. (1983). Some determinants of computer awareness among education majors. *Association for Educational Data Systems Journal, 16*, 92-103.

Hall, B. (2001). *Six steps to developing a successful e-learning initiative: Excerpts from the e-learning guidebook*. Retrieved July 10, 2003, from http://www.brandonhall .com/public/pdfs/sixstepguidebook.pdf

Harreld, J. B. (1998). Building faster, smarter organizations. In N. Kylmm (Ed.), *Blueprint for the digital economy: Creating wealth in the era of e-business*. New York: McGraw Hill.

Harrison, A. W., & Rainer, R. K., Jr. (1992). An examination of the factor structures and concurrent validities for the Computer Attitude Scale, the Computer Anxiety Scale, and the Computer Self-Efficacy Scale. *Educational and Psychological Measurement, 52*, 735-745.

Harrison, A. W., & Rainer, R. K., Jr. (1996). A general measure of user computing satisfaction. *Computers in Human Behavior, 12*(1), 79-92.

Heissen, R. K., Jr., Glass, C. R., & Knight, L. A. (1987). Assessing computer anxiety: Development and validation of the Computer Anxiety Rating Scale. *Computers in*

Human Behavior, 3, 49-59.

Howell, M. A., Vincent, J. W., & Gay, R. A. (1967). Testing aptitude for computer programming. *Psychological Reports, 20*, 1251-1256.

Jones, M. C., & Pearson, R. A. (1996). Developing an instrument to measure computer literacy. *Journal of Research on Computing in Education, 29*, 17-28.

Jones, T., & Clarke, V. A. (1994). A computer attitude scale for secondary students. *Computing in Education, 22*, 315-318.

Jorde-Bloom, P. (1988). Self-efficacy expectations as a predictor or computer use: A look at early childhood administrators. *Computers in Schools, 5*(1-2), 45-63.

Karsten, R., & Roth, R. M. (1998). The relationship of computer experience and computer self-efficacy to performance in introductory computer literacy courses. *Journal of Research on Computing in Education, 31*, 14-24.

Katz, Y. J., Evans, T., & Francis, L. J. (1995). The reliability and validity of the Hebrew version of the Bath County Computer Attitude Scale. *Journal of Educational Computing Research, 13*, 237-244.

Kay, R. H. (1989). A practical and theoretical approach to assessing computer attitudes: The Computer Attitude Measure (CAM). *Journal of Research on Computing in Education, 21*, 456-463.

Kay, R. H. (1993a). An exploration of theoretical and practical foundations for assessing attitudes toward computers: The Computer Attitude Measure (CAM). *Computers in Human Behavior, 9*, 371-386.

Kay, R. H. (1993b). A practical research tool for assessing ability to use computers: The Computer Ability Survey (CAS). *Journal of Research on Computing in Education, 26*, 16-27.

Kerlinger, F. N. (1986). *Foundations of behavioral research* (3rd ed.). New York: Hold, Rinehart, and Winston.

Kinzie, M. B., Delcourt, M. A. B., & Powers, S. M. (1994). Computer technologies: Attitudes and self-efficacy across undergraduate disciplines. *Research in Higher Education, 35*, 745-768.

Kirkpatrick, D. L. (1994). *Evaluating training programs: The four levels.* San Francisco: Berrett-Koehler.

Kluever, R., Lam, T., Hoffman, E., Green, K., & Swearingen, D. (1994). The Computer Attitude Scale: Assessing changes in teachers attitudes towards computers. *Journal of Educational Computing Research, 11*, 251-261.

Knezek, G., & Miyashita, K. T. (1994). *A preliminary study of the computer attitude questionnaire*. Denton, TX: Texan Center for Educational Technology.

Koohang, A. A. (1986). *Computerphobia: An empirical study*. Rocky Mount: North Carolina Wesleyan College. (ERIC Document Reproduction Service No. ED306948) Retrieved January 18, 2004, from the ERIC database.

Koohang, A. A. (1987). A study of the attitudes of pre-service teachers toward the use of computers. *Educational Communications and Technology Journal, 35*(3), 145-149.

Koohang, A. A. (1989). A study of attitudes toward computers: Anxiety, confidence, liking, and perception of usefulness. *Journal of Research on Computing in Education, 22*, 137-150.

Koroghlanian, C., & Brinkerhoff, J. (2000). An investigation into students pre-existing computer skills and attitudes toward Internet-delivered instruction. *Journal of Educational Technology Systems, 29*, 119-141.

Kozma, R. B. (2001). Robert Kozma's counterpoint theory of learning with media. In R. E. Clark (Ed.), *Learning from media: Arguments, analysis, and evidence* (pp. 137-178). Greenwich, CT: Information Age Publishing.

Leedy, P. D., & Ormrod, J. E. (2001). *Practical research: Planning and design* (17th ed.). Columbus, OH: Merrill Prentice Hall.

Leutner, D., & Weinsier, P. D. (1994). Attitudes toward computers and information technology at three universities in Germany, Belgium, and the U.S. *Computers in Human Behavior, 10*, 569-591.

Levine, T., & Donitsa-Schmidt, S. (1997). Commitment to learning: Effects of computer experience, confidence, and attitudes. *Journal of Educational Computing Research, 16*, 83-105.

Loyd, B. H., & Gressard, C. (1984). Reliability and factorial validity of Computer Attitude Scales. *Educational and Psychological Measurement, 44*, 501-505.

Loyd, B. H., & Gressard, C. (1986). Gender and amount of computer experience of teachers in staff development programs: Effects on computer attitudes and usefulness of computers. *Association for Educational Data Systems Journal, 18*, 302-311.

Loyd, B. H., & Loyd, D. E. (1985). The reliability and validity of an instrument for the assessment of computer attitudes. *Educational and Psychological Measurement, 45*, 903-908.

Marcoulides, G. A. (1989). Measuring computer anxiety: The Computer Anxiety Scale. *Educational and Psychological Measurement, 49*, 733-739.

Marcoulides, G. A. (1991). An examination of cross-cultural differences toward computers. *Computers in Human Behavior, 7*, 281-289.

Marcoulides, G. A., Mayes, B. T., & Wiseman, R. L. (1995). Measuring computer anxiety in the work environment. *Educational and Psychological Measurement, 55*, 804-810.

McInerney, V., Marsh, H. W., & McInerney, D. (1999). The designing of the Computer Anxiety and Learning Measure (CALM): Validation of scores on a multidimensional measure of anxiety and cognition relating to adult learning of computing skills using structural equation modeling. *Educational and Psychological Measurement, 59*, 451-470.

Milbrath, Y., & Kinzie, M. (2000). Computer technology training for prospective teachers: Computer attitudes and perceived self-efficacy. *Journal of Technology and Teacher Education, 8*, 373-396.

Miller, F., & Varma, N. (1993). The effects of psychological factors on Indian children's attitude toward computers. *Journal of Educational Computing Research, 13*, 25-29.

Molnar, A. R. (1978). The next great crisis in American education: Computer literacy. *The Journal: Technological Horizons in Education, 5*, 35-39.

Moroz, P. A., & Nash, J. B. (1997a, March 24-28). *Assessing and improving the factorial structures of the Computer Self-Efficacy Scale.* Paper presented at the Annual Meeting of the American Educational Research Association, Chicago.

Moroz, P. A., & Nash, J. B. (1997b, March 24-28). *Bath County Computer Attitude Scale: A reliability and validity scale.* Paper presented at the annual meeting of the American Educational Research Association, Chicago.

Murphy, C. A., Coover, D., & Owen, S. V. (1988, April 6-8). *Assessment of computer self-efficacy: Instrument development and validation.* Paper presented at the annual meeting of the National Council on Measurement in Education, New Orleans, LA.

National Center for Education Statistics. (1983). *Computer literacy: Definition and survey items for assessment in schools.* Washington, DC: U.S. Department of Education.

Parry, H. J., & Crossley, H. M. (1950). Validity on responses to survey questions. *Public Opinion Quarterly, 14*, 61-80.

Pelgrum, W. J., Janssen Reinen, I. A. M., & Plomp, T. J. (1993). *Schools, teachers, students, and computers: A cross-national perspective.* Twente, Netherlands: International Association for Evaluation of Educational Achievement.

Pike, N., Hofner, A., & Erlank, S. (1993). Effect of gender and occupational aspirations on attitudes towards computers. *South African Journal of Education, 13*, 25-29.

Pomazal, R. J., & Jaccard, J. J. (1976). An informational approach to altruistic behaviors. *Journal of Personality and Social Psychology, 33*, 317-326.

Popham, W. J. (1993). *Educational evaluation* (3rd ed.). Boston: Allyn and Bacon.

Pope-Davis, D. B., & Twig, J. S. (1991). The effects of age, gender, and experience on measures of attitude regarding computers. *Computers in Human Behavior, 7*, 333-339.

Poplin, M. S., Drew, D. E., & Gable, R. S. (1984). *CALIP: Computer Aptitude, Literacy, and Interest Profile*. Austin, TX: Pro-Ed.

Potosky, D., & Bobko, P. (1998). The Computer Understanding and Experience Scale: A self-report measure of computer experience. *Computers in Human Behavior, 14*, 337-348.

Raub, A. C. (1981). *Correlates of computer anxiety in college students*. Philadelphia: University of Pennsylvania.

Ravid, R. (2000). *Practical statistics for educators* (2nd ed.). Lanham, MD: University Press of America.

Reece, M. J., & Gable, R. K. (1982). The development and validation of a measure of general attitudes toward computers. *Educational and Psychological Measurement, 42*, 913-916.

Richardson, F. C., & Woolfolk, R. L. (1980). Mathematics anxiety. In I. G. Sarason (Ed.), *Test anxiety: Theory, research, and applications* (pp. 271-288). Hillsdale, NJ: Lawrence Erlbaum Associates.

Rosenberg, M. (2001). *e-Learning: Strategies for delivering knowledge in the digital age*. New York: McGraw-Hill.

Rosenberg, M. (2002). The four Cs of success: Culture, champions, communication, and change. In A. Rossett (Ed.), *The ASTD e-learning handbook* (pp. 193-217). New York: McGraw-Hill.

Rossett, A. (1999). *First things fast: A handbook for performance analysis*. San Francisco: Jossey-Bass Pfeiffer.

Rossett, A. (2002). *The ASTD e-learning handbook*. New York: McGraw-Hill.

Roszkowski, M., Devlin, S., Snelbecker, R., Aiken, R., & Jacobsohn, H. (1988). Validity and temporal stability issues regarding two measures of computer aptitudes and attitudes. *Educational and Psychological Measurement, 48*, 1029-1035.

Sanders, D. W., & Morrison-Shetlar, A. I. (2001). Student attitudes toward Web-enhanced instruction in an Introductory to Biology course. *Journal of Research on Computing in Education, 33*, 251-262.

Sarason, I. G. (1978). The Test Anxiety Scale: Concept and research. In I. G. Sarason (Ed.), *Stress and anxiety* (Vol. 5, pp. 193-218). Washington, DC: Hemisphere.

Schunk, D. H. (1984). Self-efficacy perspective on achievement behavior. *Educational Psychologist, 19*, 48-58.

Simonson, M. R., Maurer, M., Montag-Torardi, M., & Whitaker, M. (1987). Development of a standardized test of computer literacy and a computer anxiety index. *Journal of Educational Computing Research, 3*, 231-247.

Smith, B. N., & Necessary, J. R. (1996). Assessing the computer literacy of undergraduate college students. *Education, 117*, 188-193.

Snow, R. E. (1976). *Research on aptitudes: A progress report.* (Stanford University Aptitude Research Project, Technical Report No. 1). Stanford, CA: Stanford University, School of Education.

Spielberger, C. D., Gorsuch, R. L., & Lushene, R. E. (1970). State-Trait Anxiety Inventory. Palo Alto, CA: Consulting Psychologists Press.

Spooner, F., Jordan, L., Algozzine, B., & Spooner, M. (1999). Student rating of instruction in distance learning and on-campus classes. *Journal of Educational Research, 92*, 132-140.

Stevens, D. J. (1980). How educators perceive computers in the classroom. *Association for Educational Data Systems Journal, 13*, 221-232.

Stevens, D. J. (1982). Educators' perceptions of computers in education: 1979 and 1981. *Association for Educational Data Systems Journal, 16*, 1-15.

Sugrue, B. (2004). *2003 American Society for Training and Development state of the industry report.* Alexandria, VA: American Society for Training and Development.

Thompson, C., Koon, E., Woodwell, W. H., Jr., & Beauvais, J. (2002). *Training for the next economy: An ASTD state of the industry report on trends in employer-provided training in the United States for 2002.* Alexandria, VA: American Society for Training and Development.

Tull, D. S., & Albaum, G. S. (1973). *Survey research: A decisional approach.* New York: Intext Educational Publishers.

U.S. Census Bureau Public Information Office. (2002). *Demographic profiles: 100-percent and sample data.* Retrieved May 24, 2004, from thttp://www.census.gov/Press-Release/www/2002/demoprofiles.html

Urban, T., & Weggen, C. (2000). *Corporate e-learning: Exploring a new frontier.* San Francisco: WR Hambrecht and Company. Retrieved October 22, 2001, from http://www.wrhambrecht.com/research/elearning/ir/ir_explore.pdf

Woodrow, J. E. J. (1987). Educators' attitudes and predispositions towards computers. *Journal of Computers in Mathematics and Science Teaching, 6*(3), 27-37.

Woodrow, J. E. J. (1991). A comparison of four computer attitude scales. *Journal of Educational Computing Research, 7,* 165-187.

Woodrow, J. E. J. (1992). The influence of programming training on the computer literacy and attitudes of preservice teachers. *Journal of Research on Computing in Education, 25,* 200-219.

Woodrow, J. E. J. (1994). The development of computer-related attitudes of secondary students. *Journal of Educational Computing Research, 11,* 307-338.

Yacovelli, S.R. (2004). The Computer Competence, Attitude, and Behavior Scale (Version 091504). Unpublished manuscript. Unpublished manuscript, Nova Southeastern University, Fort Lauderdale, FL.

Yaghi, H. M. (1997). Pre-university students' attitudes toward computers: An international perspective. *Journal of Educational Computing Research, 16,* 237-249.

Zoltan, E., & Chapanis, A. (1982). What do professional persons think about computers. *Behavior and Information Technology, 1,* 55-68.

Appendix A

Summary of Key Findings of Literature Where Attitude Is Defined Beyond Anxiety

Summary of Key Findings of Literature Where Attitude Is Defined Beyond Anxiety

Research Dates		Total	% of
Number of Studies			26
		1980 to 2000	

Instruments Used	Total	% of Total[a]
Computer Attitude Scale (CAS) (Loyd & Gressard, 1984)	12	46
Bath County Computer Attitudes Scale (BCCAS) (Bear, Richards, & Lancaster, 1987)	7	27
Computer Use Questionnaire (Griswold, 1983)	3	19
Computers in Education Questionnaire (Stevens, 1980)	5	19
Attitudes Towards Computers (ATC) (Raub, 1981)	3	12
Attitudes Towards Computers (Reece & Gable, 1982)	3	12
Computer Attitude Measure (CAM) (Kay, 1993a)	2	8
Blomberg-Lowery Computer Attitude Task (BELCAT) (Erickson, 1987)	1	4
Computer Anxiety Rating Scale (CARS) (Heissen et al., 1987)	1	4
Computer and Information Technology Attitude Inventory (CITAI) (Leutner & Weinsier, 1994)	1	4
Computer Anxiety Index (CAIN) (Simonson et al., 1987)	1	4
Computer Attitude Items (Pelgrum et al., 1993)	1	4
Computer Attitude Questionnaire (Knezek & Miyashita, 1994)	1	4
E-Mail Survey (D'Souza, 1992)	1	4

Subjects	Total	% of Total
K-12 students		
North American K-12 students	4	15
Non-North American K-12 students	1	4
College Students		
North American college students	12	46
Non-North American college students	5	19

Adults			
	Current K-12 teachers	8	31
	Teacher faculty	2	8
	Non-academic adults	0	0

Key Trends of Literature	
	▪ Experience and Anxiety: All studies done that looked at computer anxiety and experience reviewed found a positive correlation between computer experience and positive attitude toward computers; specifically at least six months of experience using a computer reduced anxiety. Variables such as computer experience, computer usage, and mathematics anxiety were significant factors in determining overall attitude toward computers.
	▪ Gender and Anxiety: There was inconsistent data regarding gender and computer anxiety; of those that examined the issue some found that males tended to be less anxious about computers than females, while other studies reported that gender did not have a significant influence in computer attitudes.
	▪ Other Demographics: While grade level was not significant predictor to computer anxiety; age was found to significantly influence attitude toward computers. European students tend to possess a strong preference for non-computer courses as opposed to computer courses, while American students do not have a preference.
	▪ Reliability and Validity: Several studies supported the reliability and validity of the instrument being developed to measure the phenomena. In addition, multiple studies also gathered data to further support existing instruments' reliability and validity.
	▪ Scale Superiority: Of the studies that compared various measure of computer anxiety, most found little difference between the instruments' reliability and validity. However, several noted that the CAS (Loyd and Gressard, 1984) be used due to its consistency and body of research.

[a] Column totals will not add to 100% due to studies using multiple instruments and subject types.

Appendix B

Detailed Summary of Literature Where Attitude Is Defined Beyond Anxiety

Detailed Summary of Literature Where Attitude Is Defined Beyond Anxiety

Author(s)	Year	Subject(s)	Instrument(s) used	Key finding(s)
Stevens	1980	1. College students; 2. Current K-12 teachers; 3. Teacher faculty.	Computers in Education Questionnaire	Responder subgroups favored instruction to develop computer literacy; but did not feel knowledgeable enough to teach computer literacy classes.
Stevens	1982	1. College students; 2. Current K-12 teachers; 3. Teacher faculty.	Computers in Education Questionnaire	Significant increase in knowledge about computers occurred from 1980 to 1982; but no significant changes in attitudes toward computers between the two studies.
Raub	1981	College students	Attitudes Towards Computers (ATC)	1. Computer attitudes are gender-specific and culturally-learned; 2. Programming courses reduced anxiety toward computers.
Reece and Gable	1982	American 7th and 8th grade students	Attitude Toward Computers (note: different instrument from Raub, 1981)	Supported the reliability and validity of the instrument to measure students' attitudes toward computers in three domains of attitude: affective, behavioral, and cognitive.
Griswold	1983	College students	Computer Use Questionnaire	Computer application skills are needed in order to enhance computer literacy.
Woodrow	1987	1. Teachers 2. Student teachers (college students)	Computers in Education Questionnaire (modified)	1987 subjects were more positive about computers in education than Stevens' (1982) group.
Bear, Richards, and Lancaster	1987	American 4th through 12th grade students	Bath County Computer Attitudes Scale (BCCAS)	Overall attitude toward computers related to computer experience and usage, educational and career plans, choice of favorite school subject, and attitudes toward school subjects. Data supported the overall validity and reliability of the BCCAS.

Author(s)	Year	Subject(s)	Instrument(s) used	Key finding(s)
Pike, Hofner, and Erlank	1993	South African college students	Bath County Computer Attitudes Scale (BCCAS)	Students leaving school to work in the computer field had more positive attitudes toward computers than other students leaving school.
Miller and Varma	1993	Indian 7th and 8th grade students	Bath County Computer Attitudes Scale (BCCAS)	Variables of computer experiences, computer usage, and mathematics anxiety were significant factors in determining overall attitude toward computers.
Francis and Evans (1995)	1995	Welsh college students	Bath County Computer Attitudes Scale (BCCAS)	Supported the concurrent validity of the BCCAS with four other instruments purported to measure attitude toward computers (Gressard & Loyd, 1985; Griswold, 1983; Reece & Gable, 1982; Stevens, 1980).
Katz, Evans and Francis	1995	Israeli college students	Bath County Computer Attitudes Scale (BCCAS) (Hebrew version)	Findings support the overall validity and reliability of the BCCAS.
Yaghi	1997	Lebanese college students	Bath County Computer Attitudes Scale (BCCAS)	Findings support the overall validity and reliability of the BCCAS.
Leutner and Weinsier	1994	Belgium, Germany, and the United States college students	Computer and Information Technology Attitude Inventory (CITAI)	European students have a strong preference for non-computer courses as opposed to computer courses; while American students do not have a preference.
Kay	1993a	Canadian student teachers (college students)	Computer Attitude Measure (CAM)	Findings support the overall validity and reliability of the CAM.
Loyd and Gressard	1984	1. High school students 2. College students	Computer Attitude Scale (CAS)	A positive correlation between computer experience and positive attitude toward computers.

Author(s)	Year	Subject(s)	Instrument(s) used	Key finding(s)
Koohang	1986	American high school students	Computer Attitude Scale (CAS)	1. Grade level was not significant predictor to computer anxiety; 2. Males tended to be less anxious about computers than females; 3. The more computer experience, the less computer anxiety.
Pope-Davis and Twig	1991	American college students	Computer Attitude Scale (CAS)	1. Gender did not have a significant influence in computer attitudes 2. Age did significantly influence attitude toward computers; 3. Computer experience was a significant factor only on the liking subscale and not the other subscales 4. Overall the participants of the study possessed generally positive attitudes toward computers.
Loyd and Loyd	1985	American K-12 teachers	Computer Attitude Scale (CAS)	Further supported the validity of the CAS instrument, and expanded its applicability to a different population.
Koohang	1987	American K-12 teachers	Computer Attitude Scale (CAS)	There was a significant difference in overall computer experience and attitude toward computers.
Koohang	1989	American K-12 teachers	Computer Attitude Scale (CAS)	1. Gender has no significant difference on attitudes toward computers; 2. Computer experience, computer keyboarding experience, word processing, and computer programming experience do impact attitudes toward computers.

Author(s)	Year	Subject(s)	Instrument(s) used	Key finding(s)
Loyd and Gressard	1986	American teachers	Computer Attitude Scale (CAS)	1. More than one year of experience with computers were less anxious than those with less experience; 2. Males were significantly less anxious about computers than females; 3. Subjects with at least six months experience with computer perceived computers to be more useful than those with less than six months experience with computers.
Kluever, Lam, Hoffman, Green, & Swearingen	1994	American teachers	Computer Attitude Scale (CAS) (revised)	Further validated that the Computer Attitude Scale (CAS) is a reliable instrument in the measurement of teacher attitudes toward computers.
Woodrow	1991	College students	Computer Attitude Scale (Loyd & Gressard, 1984), Computer Use Questionnaire (Griswold, 1983), Attitudes Toward Computers (Reece & Gable, 1982), and Computer Survey (Stevens, 1980)	1. Found overall the four scales were very similar; 2. Suggested the use of the CAS (Loyd and Gressard, 1984) because of its consistency and body of research
Gardner, Discenza, and Dukes	1993	College students	Attitudes Towards Computers (ATC) (Raub, 1981); Computer Attitudes Scale (CAS) (Loyd & Gressard, 1984); Computer Anxiety Index (CAIN) (Simonson et al., 1987); Blomberg-Lowery Computer Attitude Task, or BELCAT (Erickson, 1987)	Found that all four instruments were "…essentially equal in terms of reliability and validity," (Gardner et al,, 1993, p.487).
Moroz and Nash	1997b	American graduate students	Bath County Computer Attitude Scale (BCCAS) (Bear, Richards and Lancaster, 1987); Computer Attitude Scale (Loyd & Loyd, 1985)	The BCCAS was internally consistent and predicative of a range of attitudinal domains towards computers.

156

Author(s)	Year	Subject(s)	Instrument(s) used	Key finding(s)
Christensen and Knezek	2000	American teachers (in Texas, Florida, New York, and California)	CAS (Gressard & Loyd, 1985); Computer Use Questionnaire (Griswold, 1983); ATC (Reece & Gable, 1982); Computer Survey Scale (Stevens, 1980); CARS (Heissen et al., 1987); ATC (Raub, 1981); BELCAT (Erickson, 1987); ACTS (Francis, 1993); CAM (Kay, 1993a); Computer Attitude Questionnaire (Knezek & Miyashita, 1994); Computer Attitude Items (Pelgrum et al., 1993); CASS (Jones & Clarke, 1994); E-Mail (D'Souza, 1992)	1. Most of the instruments' that originally had higher internal consistency reliabilities remained close to the same levels; 2. Loyd and Gressard's CSA instrument (1984), slightly decreased from 0.86 in 1986 to 0.75 in 1995 (but this is still a respectable level).

Appendix C

Summary of Key Findings of Literature That Examined Computer Literacy,

Competence, and Aptitude

Summary of Key Findings of Literature That Examined Computer Literacy, Competence, and Aptitude

Research Dates		1980 to 1998	
Number of Studies			10

Instruments		Total	% of Total[a]
Used	Computer Self-Efficacy Scale (CSE) (Murphy, Coover, & Owen, 1988)	3	30
	Minnesota Computer Literacy and Awareness Assessment (Anderson, Krohn, & Sandman, 1980)	2	20
	Standardized Test for Computer Literacy (Simonson, Maurer, Montag-Torardi & Whitaker, 1987)	1	10
	Computer Ability Survey (CAS) (Kay, 1993b)	1	10
	Computer Understanding and Experience (CUE) Scale (Potosky & Bobko, 1998)	1	10
	Unnamed instrument (Gabriel, 1985)	1	10
	Unnamed instrument (Jones & Pearson, 1996)	1	10
Subjects			
	K-12 students		
	North American K-12 students	3	30
	Non-North American K-12 students	0	0
	College Students		
	North American college students	6	60
	Non-North American college students	1	10
	Adults		
	Current K-12 teachers	1	10
	Teacher faculty	0	0
	Non-academic adults	2	20

Key Trends of Literature	■ Computer literacy and attitudes: All studies reviewed which looked at both computer literacy and attitudes toward computers showed a positive correlation between average attitudes toward computers and the average level of self-reported computer competence.
	■ Computer literacy and experience: There was a discrepancy between the correlation between computer literacy and experience; while several studies reported a positive correlation between the increase of computer literacy and the amount of "hands-on" computer experience, one other noted that relevance of computer experience is most predictive of performance, not the amount of computer experience or exposure.
	■ Mathematic ability and computer literacy: Studies showed a positive correlation between the self-reported computer competence and mathematical ability.
	■ Gender and computer literacy: The studies reviewed did not have clear findings regarding gender and computer literacy; in one study females performed better than their male counterparts in some specific areas of computer programming where problems are verbal versus mathematic; while another study noted that overall males and females have varying degrees of self-reported computer skills with males being more "computer literate" as self-reported.
	■ Reliability and Validity: Several studies supported the reliability and validity of the instrument being developed to measure the phenomena.

Appendix D

Detailed Summary of Literature That Examined Computer Literacy,

Competence, and Aptitude

Detailed Summary of Literature That Examined Computer Literacy, Competence, and Aptitude

Author(s)	Year	Subject(s)	Instrument(s) used	Key finding(s)
Anderson, Krohn, & Sandman	1980	K-12 students	Minnesota Computer Literacy and Awareness Assessment	1. Females high school students performed better than their male counterparts in some specific areas of computer programming where problems are verbal versus mathematic; 2. Overall evidence was found to support the MCLAA's construct validity.
Bitter & Davis	1985	American teachers	Minnesota Computer Literacy and Awareness Assessment	1. Participants' overall attitudes toward computers remained fairly consistent over the 2 year study; 2. Overall teachers were knowledgeable about computers as measured by the MCCLAA 3. Subjects has a positive correlation between average attitudes toward computers and the average level of computer knowledge.
Gabriel	1985	1. Grades 4, 7 and 11 students in Department of Defense Dependents School (DoDDS) system; 2. American K-12 students.	Unnamed instrument	1. General problem solving skills declined after the first tier (4th Grade); 2. Positive correlation between the increase of computer literacy and the amount of "hands-on" time; 3. Essentially the same pattern existed between DoDDS and American K-12 subjects.
Simonson, Maurer, Montag-Torardi & Whitaker	1987	American college students	Standardized Test for Computer Literacy	1. Subjects thought the instrument did measure computer literacy; 2. Data supported the overall reliability and validity of the instrument.
Murphy, Coover, & Owen	1988	1. Graduate students; 2. Nurses.	Computer Self-Efficacy Scale (CSE)	1. Males and females have varying degrees of self-reported computer skills; 2. Overall data supported the validity and reliability of the instrument.

Author(s)	Year	Subject(s)	Instrument(s) used	Key finding(s)
Karsten & Roth	1998	College students	Computer Self-Efficacy Scale (CSE)	1. Relevance of computer experience is most predictive of performance, not the amount of computer experience or exposure. 2. Computer self-efficacy is significantly related to computer-dependent course performance.
Moroz & Nash	1997a	College students	Computer Self-Efficacy Scale (CSE) (revised version)	1. The new instrument is measuring the same construct to a similar degree for high and low computer users. 2. The instrument is suitable for measuring computer self-efficacy.
Kay	1993b	Canadian pre-service teachers (college students)	Computer Ability Survey (CAS)	1. Positive correlations exist between all the computer ability subscales and mathematical ability, attitudes toward computers, and an independent measure of software ability 2. Data supported the overall validity and reliability of the instrument.
Jones & Pearson	1996	College students	Unnamed instrument	1. Subjects tended to have low self-reported computer competence; consistent with the other two administration of the instrument; 2. The "I don't know" option in the instrument improves overall validity of the instrument.
Potosky & Bobko	1998	1. American college students 2. Full-time computer programmers	Computer Understanding and Experience (CUE) Scale	1. Data supported the overall validity and reliability of the instrument.

Appendix E

Summary of Key Findings of Literature That Examined Both Attitudes Toward

Computers and Computer Literacy

Summary of Key Findings of Literature That Examined Both Attitudes Toward Computers and Computer Literacy

Research Dates			1988 to 2000
Number of Studies			7
Instruments		Total	% of Total[a]
Used	Computer Attitude Scale (Loyd & Gressard, 1984)	4	57
	Attitudes Toward Computer Technologies (ACT) (Delcourt & Kinzie, 1993)	2	29
	Self-Efficacy with Computer Technologies (SCT) (Delcourt & Kinzie, 1993)	2	29
	Attitude Toward Computers (Reece & Gable, 1982)	2	29
	Computer Aptitude, Literacy, & Interest Profile (Poplin, Drew, & Gable; 1984)	1	14
	Minnesota Computer Literacy and Awareness Assessment (Anderson et al., 1980)	1	14
	Computer Literacy and Awareness Assessment (Anderson et al., 1980)	1	14
	Computer Survey (Koohang, 1987)	1	14
	Computer Anxiety Rating Scale (Heissen, Glass & Knight, 1987)	1	14
	Computer Self-Efficacy Scale (Murphy, Coover & Owen, 1988)	1	14
	Computer-Ability Gender Equality (Woodrow, 1992)	1	14
	Computer Ability Scale (Kay, 1993a)	1	14
	Computer Attitude Measure (Kay, 1993b)	1	14
	Computer Survey Instrument (Stevens, 1980, 1982)	1	14
Subjects			
	K-12 students	0	0
	North American K-12 students	0	0
	Non-North American K-12 students	0	0
	College Students	6	86
	North American college students	6	86
	Non-North American college students	0	0

Adults	3	43
Current K-12 teachers	2	29
Teacher faculty	0	0
Non-academic adults	1	14

Key Trends of Literature	<ul><li>Computer literacy and experience: All studies that looked at experience and computer literacy reviewed by the author found a positive correlation between frequency of use and self-reported computer aptitude.</li><li>Computer literacy and attitudes: As expected, studies that looked at the correlation between these two phenomena noted that attitudes were statistically significant predictors of self-efficacy; conversely high anxiety correlated with negative feelings toward computers and lower self-reported computer skill level, and subjects' attitudes were positively correlated with achievement in the programming course with the exception of the gender-ability dimension.</li><li>Gender and computer literacy and attitude toward computers: Again, the studies reviewed did not have clear findings regarding gender and computer literacy; one study noted that males scored significantly higher in their attitude toward computers than females while another found no significant difference between gender and the two phenomena.</li></ul>

[a] Column totals will not add to 100% due to studies using multiple instruments and subject types.

Appendix F

Detailed Summary of Literature That Examined Both Attitudes Toward

Computers and Computer Literacy

Detailed Summary of Literature that Examined Both Attitudes Toward Computers and Computer Literacy

Author(s)	Year	Subject(s)	Instrument(s) used	Key finding(s)
Roszkowski, Devlin, Snelbecker, Aiken, & Jacobsohn	1988	Teachers	1. Computer Aptitude, Literacy, & Interest Profile (Poplin, Drew, & Gable; 1984) 2. Computer Attitude Scale (Loyd & Gressard, 1984)	1. The CAS was shown to exhibit comparable validity to the CALIP
Woodrow	1992	Pre-service teachers (college students)	1. Computer Literacy and Awareness Assessment (Anderson et al., 1980); 2. Computer Attitude Scale (Loyd & Gressard, 1984); 3. Attitude Toward Computers (Reece & Gable, 1982); 4. Computer Survey instrument (Stevens, 1980, 1982); 5. Computer-Ability Gender Equality by the author	1. Subjects' attitudes were positively correlated with achievement in the programming course with the exception of the gender-ability dimension; 2. No significant changes in neither relationship to gender in entry-level computer attitudes nor toward the attitudes of computers.
Woodrow	1994	Pre-service teachers (college students)	1. Computer Attitude Scale (Loyd & Gressard, 1984); 2. Attitudes Toward Computers (Reece & Gable, 1982); 3. Minnesota Computer Literacy and Awareness Assessment (Anderson et al., 1980); 4. Computer Survey (Koohang, 1987)	1. The greatest variance in attitudes toward computers occurred through unstructured computer experience and word processing experience; 2. While gains in computer attitudes were independent of gender, computer training experience and computer course achievement.
Harrison & Rainer	1992	Adults working at an American university	1. Computer Attitude Scale (Loyd & Gressard, 1984); 2. Computer Anxiety Rating Scale (Heissen, Glass & Knight, 1987); 3. Computer Self-Efficacy Scale (Murphy, Coover & Owen, 1988).	1. High anxiety correlated with negative feelings toward computers and lower self-reported computer skill level; 2. Higher confidence correlated with positive attitudes and higher self-reported computer skills.

Author(s)	Year	Subject(s)	Instrument(s) used	Key finding(s)
Delcourt & Kinzie	1993	1. American teacher education undergraduate students; 2. American graduate students; 3. American teachers.	1. Attitudes Toward Computer Technologies (ACT) by authors; 2. Self-Efficacy with Computer Technologies (SCT) by authors.	Attitudes were statistically significant predictors of self-efficacy for all three types of computer technologies (word processing, e-mail, and CD-ROM database usage).
Milbrath & Kinzie	2000	Pre-service teachers (college students)	1. Attitudes Toward Computer Technologies (Delcourt & Kinzie, 1993); 2. Self-Efficacy with Computer Technologies (Delcourt & Kinzie, 1993);	More frequent use of various facets of computers (word processing, spreadsheet usage, etc.) would yield high self-efficacy and comfort with that particular facet of computer technology
Smith & Necessary	1996	College students	1. Computer Ability Scale (Kay, 1993a); 2. Computer Attitude Measure (Kay, 1993b).	1. Similar findings to original study (Kay, 1993a; 1993b): males scored significantly higher in their attitude toward computers than females 2. Positive correlation between years of computer use and higher self-reported computer ability; 3. Positive correlation between more frequent weekly use of a computer and higher self-reported computer aptitude.

Appendix G

Summary of Key Findings of Literature That Examined Attitudes Toward End-User

Software and Multimedia Instruction or e-Learning

Summary of Key Findings of Literature That Examined Attitudes Toward End-User Software and Multimedia Instruction or e-Learning

		Total	% of Total[a]
Research Dates			1988 to 2001
Number of Studies			6
Instruments			
Used	End-User Computing Satisfaction Instrument (EUCSI) (Harrison & Rainer, 1996)	2	33
	Multimedia Attitude Survey (MAS) (Coll Garcia, 2001)	1	17
	Unnamed student evaluation instrument (Spooner, Jordan, Algozzine, & Spooner, 1999)	1	17
	Unnamed survey (Koroghlanian & Brinkerhoff, 2000)	1	17
	Web-based Instruction Attitude Scale (Sanders & Morrison-Shetlar, 2001)	1	17
Subjects			
K-12 students			
	North American K-12 students	0	0
	Non-North American K-12 students	0	0
College Students			
	North American college students	3	50
	Non-North American college students	1	17
Adults			
	Current K-12 teachers	0	0
	Teacher faculty	0	0
	Non-academic adults	2	33

Key Trends of Literature

- Attitudes toward e-Learning: Students with prior Internet instruction experience far less optimistic concerning the degree to which technology may interfere with learning; and students with prior e-learning experience were more likely to recommend taking an Internet-delivered course.

- Demographics and Attitudes toward e-Learning: While the analysis between gender and attitudes toward e-learning was only done in one study reviewed in the literature, the researchers discovered females were significantly more positive toward the use of the Web-based instructional component than males; and females used the Internet more frequently than males. In addition, no significant correlation was found between ethnicity, year in school, age, or computer experience and attitudes toward the Web-based instruction.

- ▪ Reliability and Validity: Several studies supported the reliability and validity of the instrument being developed to measure the phenomena.

[a] Column totals will not add to 100% due to studies using multiple instruments and subject types.

Appendix H

Detailed Summary of Literature That Examined Attitudes Toward End-User Software

and Multimedia Instruction or e-Learning

Detailed Summary of Literature that Examined Attitudes Toward End-User Software and Multimedia Instruction or e-Learning

Author(s)	Year	Subject(s)	Instrument(s) used	Key finding(s)
Doll & Torkzadeh	1988	Corporate adults	End User Computing Satisfaction Instrument (EUCSI)	Data supports the overall validity and reliability of the instrument.
Harrison & Rainer	1996	Adults	End User Computing Satisfaction Instrument (EUCSI)	Data further supports the overall validity and reliability of the instrument.
Spooner, Jordan, Algozzine, & Spooner	1999	College students	Unnamed student evaluation instrument	No difference in overall satisfaction between electronic and face-to-face course delivery methods
Koroghlanian & Brinkerhoff	2000	College students	Unnamed survey developed by the authors	1. Student computer skills were relatively shallow; consisting of basic software skills; 2. Students were generally neutral toward Internet-based instruction; 3. Students with prior Internet instruction experience far less optimistic concerning the degree to which technology may interfere with learning; 4. Students with prior experience were more likely to recommend taking an Internet-delivered course.
Coll Garcia	2001	Spanish college students	Multimedia Attitude Survey (MAS)	Data from pilot study supports the overall validity and reliability of the instrument
Sanders & Morrison-Shetlar	2001	College students	Web-based Instruction Attitude Scale	1. Females were significantly more positive toward the use of the Web-based instructional component than males; 2. Females used the Internet more frequently than males; 3. No significant correlation was found between ethnicity, year in school, age, or computer experience and attitudes toward the Web-based instruction.

Appendix I

CCABS: Computer Competence, Attitude, and Behavior Scale

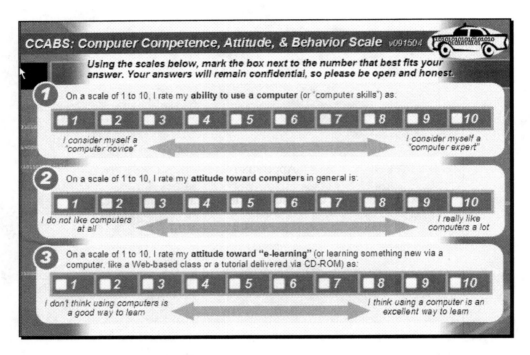

Note. From Computer Competence, Attitude, and Behavior Scale (Version 091504) by S. Yacovelli, 2004, unpublished manuscript, Nova Southeastern University, Fort Lauderdale, FL.

Appendix J

The Regan CCABS

The Regan Computer Competence, Attitude, & Behavior Survey

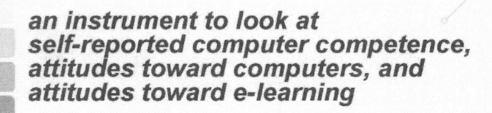

an instrument to look at self-reported computer competence, attitudes toward computers, and attitudes toward e-learning

v093004

The Regan Computer Competence, Attitude, & Behavior Survey v093004

1 First: Tell Us About You ...

This section asks for some information about you.
Please remember that your responses are completely anonymous.

1. My age is ...
   (check one)

☐	☐	☐	☐	☐	☐	☐	☐	☐	☐	☐	☐	☐
<18	18-24	25-29	30-34	35-39	40-44	45-49	50-54	55-59	60-64	65-69	70-74	75+

2. My gender is ...   ☐ Male   ☐ Female

3. The 5-digit ZIP code where I live is ...   ☐ ☐ ☐ ☐ ☐

4. What is the highest degree or level of school you have completed?

   ☐ No High School diploma   ☐ Associate degree   ☐ Professional degree
   　　　　　　　　　　　　　　　　　　　　(for example: AA, AS)   *(for example: MD, DDS, DVM, LLB, JD)*

   ☐ High School diploma or
   　 equivalent   ☐ Bachelor's degree   ☐ Doctorate degree
   　 (for example: GED)   *(for example: BA, AB, BS)*   *(for example: PhD, EdD)*

   ☐ 1 or more years of   ☐ Master's degree
   　 college, no degree   *(for example: MA, MS, MEng, MEd, MSW, MBA)*

5. I am classified as working in the following area: ☐ Hourly   ☐ Salaried   ☐ Other: _____
   　　　(please specify)

6. I have been with this company
   for _____ years   ☐ 0-1   ☐ 2-4   ☐ 5-9   ☐ 10-14   ☐ 15-19   ☐ 20-25   ☐ 25+

7. I have taken a course or training class delivered via the Internet.   ☐ Yes   ☐ No   ☐ I'm not sure

2 Now: Tell Us About Your Organization ...

Please tell us a little about the organization with which you are affiliated.

8. Number of employees in your   ☐ 1 to 100   ☐ 101 to 500   ☐ 501 to 1,000   ☐ 1,001 to 5,000   ☐ 5,000+
   organization:

9. Which describes your organization or affiliation?

   ☐ Government Organization   ☐ Higher Education   ☐ Large Business (1,000+ employees)   ☐ Small Business
   ☐ Home Office   ☐ Primary / Secondary   ☐ Medium Business   　 (1 – 99 employees)
   　　　　　　　　　　　　　　　　 Education   　 (100 – 999 employees)   ☐ Other

10. Which best describes your organization's industry?

☐ Advertising / Marketing / Public Relations	☐ Finance / Insurance / Real Estate	☐ Healthcare / Pharmaceutical / Biotech	☐ Media / Entertainment / Arts	☐ Non-Profit / Charity	☐ Software / Hardware / Tele-communications	☐ Web / IT Professional Services
☐ Education	☐ Government / Military / Aerospace	☐ Manufacturing / Research & Development	☐ Non-IT Professional Services / Legal	☐ Retail / Wholesale / Trade	☐ Travel / Transportation / Hospitality	☐ Workforce Development / Professional Training
☐ Other						

continued to next section ➡

3 What Do You Know about Computers?

This sections looks at your knowledge around computers and computer technology. THERE ARE NO "RIGHT" OR "WRONG" ANSWERS! **Circle the response that best fits** with whether you *Strongly Disagree (SD)* with the sentence, or if you *Strongly Agree (SA)* with it. *EXAMPLE:* I like the color green.   SD D DA (A) SA

SCALE:
SD = *Strongly Disagree,* **D** = *Disagree,* **DA** = *Sometimes Disagree/Agree,* **A** = *Agree,* **SA** = *Strongly Agree*

11.	I own a computer.	SD	D	DA	A	SA
12.	I am good at using computers	SD	D	DA	A	SA
13.	I know what an operating system is	SD	D	DA	A	SA
14.	I know what a database is	SD	D	DA	A	SA
15.	I know how to install software on a personal computer	SD	D	DA	A	SA
16.	I know how to write computer programs	SD	D	DA	A	SA
17.	I know what a LAN is	SD	D	DA	A	SA
18.	I often use a mainframe computer system	SD	D	DA	A	SA
19.	I know how to recover deleted or "lost data" on a computer	SD	D	DA	A	SA
20.	I have Internet access at home	SD	D	DA	A	SA
21.	When I come across a topic I do not know or understand, I first consult the Internet for information	SD	D	DA	A	SA
22.	I am comfortable with on-line business transactions (like checking my bank statements or paying my credit card bills on-line)	SD	D	DA	A	SA
23.	I have purchased something through the Internet (like airline tickets, movie tickets, items bought through eBay®)	SD	D	DA	A	SA
24.	I have used a computer for learning something new (like finding a new recipe or how to fix a broken VCR)	SD	D	DA	A	SA
25.	I know what e-mail is	SD	D	DA	A	SA
26.	I have a personal e-mail account	SD	D	DA	A	SA
27.	I use e-mail more often to communicate with family and friends than I do through standard letters	SD	D	DA	A	SA
28.	I have participated in a "chat room"	SD	D	DA	A	SA
29.	I regularly use a PC or computer for word processing	SD	D	DA	A	SA
30.	I have used an Automated Teller Machine (ATM)	SD	D	DA	A	SA
31.	I know how to save and print pictures from a digital camera	SD	D	DA	A	SA
32.	I use a Palm Pilot® or other type of Personal Digital Assistant (PDA) frequently	SD	D	DA	A	SA
33.	I frequently read computer magazines or other sources of information that describe new computer technology	SD	D	DA	A	SA
34.	I consider myself to be computer literate	SD	D	DA	A	SA
35.	I am comfortable ... reading, sending and deleting e-mail messages	SD	D	DA	A	SA
36.	I am comfortable ... sending and reading e-mail attachments	SD	D	DA	A	SA
37.	I am comfortable ... following threaded discussions and posting messages on bulletin boards on the computer	SD	D	DA	A	SA
38.	I am comfortable ... participating in chat sessions	SD	D	DA	A	SA

continued ➡

2

The Regan Computer Competence, Attitude, & Behavior Survey v093004

3 What Do You Know about Computers? *(continued)*

SCALE:
SD = *Strongly Disagree*, **D** = *Disagree*, **DA** = *Sometimes Disagree/Agree*, **A** = *Agree*, **SA** = *Strongly Agree*

39.	I am comfortable ... installing the latest version of a browser such as Internet Explorer® or Netscape®	SD	D	DA	A	SA
40.	I am comfortable ... locating and installing plugins such as Shockwave®, Quicktime®, Flash®, or VRML	SD	D	DA	A	SA
41.	I am comfortable ... creating Web pages with images, links, and text	SD	D	DA	A	SA
42.	I am comfortable ... following links on Web pages and returning to the starting point	SD	D	DA	A	SA
43.	I am comfortable ... recognizing clickable objects on Web pages	SD	D	DA	A	SA
44.	I am comfortable ... downloading files embedded on Web pages	SD	D	DA	A	SA
45.	I am comfortable ... knowing what a "PDF" file is	SD	D	DA	A	SA
46.	I am comfortable ... opening files with Adobe Acrobat®	SD	D	DA	A	SA
47.	I am comfortable ... printing one or more pages from Adobe Acrobat®	SD	D	DA	A	SA
48.	I am comfortable ... opening a compressed file (sometimes called a ZIP file)	SD	D	DA	A	SA
49.	I am comfortable ... moving files to different drives within my computer	SD	D	DA	A	SA
50.	Overall, I would consider myself to be competent with computers	SD	D	DA	A	SA

continued to next section ▶

4 What Do You Think about Computers?

This sections looks at your opinions around computers and the people who use them. THERE ARE NO "RIGHT" OR "WRONG" ANSWERS! **Circle the response that best fits** with whether you *Strongly Disagree (SD)* with the sentence, or if you *Strongly Agree (SA)* with it.

SCALE:
SD = *Strongly Disagree*, **D** = *Disagree*, **DA** = *Sometimes Disagree/Agree*, **A** = *Agree*, **SA** = *Strongly Agree*

51.	Computers do not scare me at all	SD	D	DA	A	SA
52.	I get anxious when I think of trying to use a computer	SD	D	DA	A	SA
53.	I'm no good with computers	SD	D	DA	A	SA
54.	I am sure I could learn a computer language	SD	D	DA	A	SA
55.	It wouldn't bother me at all to take computer courses	SD	D	DA	A	SA
56.	Computers make me feel uncomfortable	SD	D	DA	A	SA
57.	Working with a computer would make me very nervous	SD	D	DA	A	SA
58.	I would feel at ease in a computer class	SD	D	DA	A	SA
59.	I would feel comfortable working with a computer	SD	D	DA	A	SA
60.	I'm not the type to do well with computers	SD	D	DA	A	SA
61.	I do not feel threatened when others talk about computers	SD	D	DA	A	SA
62.	Generally, I would feel OK about trying a new problem on the computer	SD	D	DA	A	SA
63.	I don't think I would do advanced computer work	SD	D	DA	A	SA

continued ▶

4 What Do You Think about Computers? *(continued)*

SCALE:
SD = *Strongly Disagree,* **D** = *Disagree,* **DA** = *Sometimes Disagree/Agree,* **A** = *Agree,* **SA** = *Strongly Agree*

		SD	D	DA	A	SA
64.	Computers make me feel uneasy and confused	SD	D	DA	A	SA
65.	I am sure I could do work with computers	SD	D	DA	A	SA
66.	I feel aggressive and hostile toward computers	SD	D	DA	A	SA
67.	I think using a computer would be very hard for me	SD	D	DA	A	SA
68.	I would be successful in computer training courses	SD	D	DA	A	SA
69.	I do not think I could handle a computer training course	SD	D	DA	A	SA
70.	I have a lot of self-confidence when it comes to working with computers	SD	D	DA	A	SA
71.	I would like working with computers	SD	D	DA	A	SA
72.	The challenge of solving problems with computers does not appeal to me	SD	D	DA	A	SA
73.	I think working with computers would be enjoyable and stimulating	SD	D	DA	A	SA
74.	Figuring out computer problems does not appeal to me	SD	D	DA	A	SA
75.	When there is a problem with a computer run that I can't immediately solve, I would "stick with it" until I have the answer	SD	D	DA	A	SA
76.	I don't understand how some people can spend so much time working with computers and seem to enjoy it	SD	D	DA	A	SA
77.	Once I start to work with the computer, I would find it hard to stop	SD	D	DA	A	SA
78.	I do as little work with computers as possible	SD	D	DA	A	SA
79.	If a problem is left unsolved in a computer training class, I would continue to think about it afterward	SD	D	DA	A	SA
80.	I do not enjoy talking with others about computers	SD	D	DA	A	SA
81.	I use computers many ways in my life	SD	D	DA	A	SA
82.	Learning about computers is a waste of time	SD	D	DA	A	SA
83.	Learning about computers is worthwhile	SD	D	DA	A	SA
84.	I need a firm mastery of computers for my work	SD	D	DA	A	SA
85.	I have little use for computers in my daily life	SD	D	DA	A	SA
86.	I can't think of any way that I use computers in my career	SD	D	DA	A	SA
87.	Knowing how to work with computers increases my job possibilities	SD	D	DA	A	SA
88.	Anything that a computer can be used for, I can do just as well some other way	SD	D	DA	A	SA
89.	It is important to me to do well in computer training courses	SD	D	DA	A	SA
90.	Working with computers is not important to me in my life's work	SD	D	DA	A	SA
91.	Computers cause more trouble than they are worth	SD	D	DA	A	SA
92.	People who don't know how to use a computer cannot function in modern society	SD	D	DA	A	SA

continued ➡

4

182

The Regan Computer Competence, Attitude, & Behavior Survey v093004

4. What Do You Think about Computers? *(continued)*

SCALE:
SD = *Strongly Disagree*, **D** = *Disagree*, **DA** = *Sometimes Disagree/Agree*, **A** = *Agree*, **SA** = *Strongly Agree*

#		SD	D	DA	A	SA
93.	I find computers to be vital to my everyday life	SD	D	DA	A	SA
94.	I enjoy working on a computer	SD	D	DA	A	SA
95.	Computers are too difficult to use	SD	D	DA	A	SA
96.	I usually get frustrated using a computer	SD	D	DA	A	SA
97.	I can use a computer to accomplish what I want	SD	D	DA	A	SA
99.	I feel computers are valuable tools in people's personal and professional lives	SD	D	DA	A	SA
99.	Computers serve little use in my life	SD	D	DA	A	SA
100.	I think computers are better left used by office workers and "younger" people	SD	D	DA	A	SA

continued to next section ➡

5. What Do You Think about Internet-Delivered Training?

This sections looks at your opinions around using the computer for training. THERE ARE NO "RIGHT" OR "WRONG" ANSWERS! **Circle the response that best fits** with whether you *Strongly Disagree (SD)* with the sentence, or if you *Strongly Agree (SA)* with it.

SCALE:
SD = *Strongly Disagree*, **D** = *Disagree*, **DA** = *Sometimes Disagree/Agree*, **A** = *Agree*, **SA** = *Strongly Agree*

#		SD	D	DA	A	SA
101.	I am sure I could do well in an Internet-delivered course	SD	D	DA	A	SA
102.	I am not the type to do well with computers	SD	D	DA	A	SA
103.	Taking an Internet-delivered training class would be one way to stay current with new technology	SD	D	DA	A	SA
104.	Internet-delivered training classes provide an efficient way for me to utilize my time	SD	D	DA	A	SA
105.	I would be upset if a required training class were only offered over the Internet	SD	D	DA	A	SA
106.	I feel at ease using the Internet (or "Web")	SD	D	DA	A	SA
107.	I feel that technology gets in the way of learning content	SD	D	DA	A	SA
108.	If I had a choice between taking an Internet training class or a "traditional" face to face section of the same class, I would choose the Internet section	SD	D	DA	A	SA
109.	If I took a training class delivered over the Internet, I would feel isolated	SD	D	DA	A	SA
110.	I feel that Internet-delivered training classes provide a greater opportunity for interactivity between students, and between students and instructor	SD	D	DA	A	SA
111.	I would be anxious about taking an Internet-delivered training class	SD	D	DA	A	SA
112.	I would be excited to take a training class delivered over the Internet	SD	D	DA	A	SA
113.	If I took a training class delivered via the Internet, it would be a chance to learn about the Internet	SD	D	DA	A	SA

continued ➡

The Regan Computer Competence, Attitude, & Behavior Survey v093004

5 What Do You Think about Internet-Delivered Training?

This sections looks at your opinions around using the computer for training.
THERE ARE NO "RIGHT" OR "WRONG" ANSEWERS! **Circle the response that best fits** with whether you *Strongly Disagree (SD)* with the sentence, or if you *Strongly Agree (SA)* with it.

SCALE:
SD = *Strongly Disagree,* **D** = *Disagree,* **DA** = *Sometimes Disagree/Agree,* **A** = *Agree,* **SA** = *Strongly Agree*

114.	I feel that Internet-delivered training classes are impersonal	SD	D	DA	A	SA
115.	Access would be a problem if I took an Internet-delivered training class	SD	D	DA	A	SA
116.	Taking an Internet-delivered training class would be a good way to learn	SD	D	DA	A	SA
117.	It would be convenient for me to take an Internet-delivered training class	SD	D	DA	A	SA
118.	I think using a computer for a training class would be very hard for me	SD	D	DA	A	SA
119.	I would find it hard to motivate myself if I were to take a training class using the Internet	SD	D	DA	A	SA
120.	Internet-delivered training classes are an efficient way to deliver training	SD	D	DA	A	SA
121.	It's better to attend a training class with an instructor than gain the same information from a computer	SD	D	DA	A	SA
122.	I could learn just as well from an Internet-delivered course as I could from a "traditional" training class	SD	D	DA	A	SA
123.	I would like the flexibility of attending an Internet-delivered training class	SD	D	DA	A	SA
124.	Communicating online with classmates in Internet-delivered courses would be an enhancement to learning	SD	D	DA	A	SA
125.	I would feel uneasy if I had to take an Internet-delivered training class	SD	D	DA	A	SA
126.	Training delivered over the Internet is too impersonal	SD	D	DA	A	SA
127.	I feel an Internet-delivered training course would allow more interaction between students, and between the students and the teacher	SD	D	DA	A	SA
128.	The use of technology can enhance the learning in a training course	SD	D	DA	A	SA
129.	I would be eager to take a training class delivered over the Internet	SD	D	DA	A	SA
130.	If I were to take a training class delivered over the Internet, I would find it hard to complete the class	SD	D	DA	A	SA
131.	When given the choice, I choose to take this survey on paper because:					

Survey complete. Thank you for your time and honesty!

About this Survey ...

This survey is comprised of questions from both previously developed instruments, some slightly modified, and newly developed instruments. These include:

- *Computer Attitude Scale* (1984) by Loyd & Gressard
- *Computer Understanding & Experience Scale* (1998) by Potosky & Bobko
- *Unnamed Instrument* (2000) by Koroghlanian & Brinkerhoff
- *Regan Demographic Survey* (2004) by Yacovelli
- *Regan Technology Behavior Survey* (2004) by Yacovelli

Permission was obtained to use the existing instruments for the creation of *The Regan Computer Competence, Attitude, & Behavior Survey*. Its development is partial fulfillment of the requirements for the degree of Doctor of Education at Nova Southeastern University, Ft. Lauderdale, Florida, USA.

The Regan Computer Competence, Attitude, & Behavior Survey
v093004

Note. From The Regan Computer Competence, Attitude, and Behavior Scale (Version 093004) by S. Yacovelli, unpublished manuscript, Nova Southeastern University, Fort Lauderdale, FL.

Appendix K

Subject Matter Expert Feedback Form

Information Packet for Subject Matter Experts' Review.

SME FEEDBACK SHEET

Your Name	_____
Title	_____
Organization	_____
Phone	( ) ---

PLEASE FAX TO STEVE @ (321) 206-0833
BY WEDNESDAY DECEMBER 18, 2004. THANK YOU FOR YOUR HELP!

FACE VALIDITY:

In your opinion, is this instrument a representative sample of the domain of:

    1.   Employee Attitudes toward Computers

☐1 ☐2 ☐3 ☐4 ☐5 ☐6 ☐7 ☐8 ☐9 ☐10

Does not seem to contain a   ⟷   Seems to accurately contain a
representative sample of   representative sample of
the domain   the domain

    2.   Employee Self-Report Computer Aptitude

☐1 ☐2 ☐3 ☐4 ☐5 ☐6 ☐7 ☐8 ☐9 ☐10

Does not seem to contain a   ⟷   Seems to accurately contain a
representative sample of   representative sample of
the domain   the domain

    3.   Employee Attitudes toward e-Learning

☐1 ☐2 ☐3 ☐4 ☐5 ☐6 ☐7 ☐8 ☐9 ☐10

Does not seem to contain a   ⟷   Seems to accurately contain a
representative sample of   representative sample of
the domain   the domain

(continued)

187

Content Validity

Another facet of establishing the validity of the instrument is through *Content Validity*; the degree to which an instrument is a representative sample of the content area (or domain) being measured. One tactic noted in the literature is using folks like you to evaluate the instrument's overall content validity.

In the spaces provided below, please evaluate the three sections of *Regan Computer Attitude, Aptitude, and Behavior Survey*, based upon your perception of how it measures the three domains or phenomena being examined.

Section 3 – Self-Reported Computer Competence

Section 4 – Attitudes Toward Computers

Section 5 – Attitudes Toward Internet-Delivered Training

Appendix L

Adult Consent Form

NOVA SOUTHEASTERN UNIVERSITY
Fischler Graduate School of Education
and Human Services

**Adult/General Consent for Participation in
The Development and Use of an Instrument to Measure Adult Learner's
Perceived Levels of Computer Competence, Attitudes Toward Computers,
and Attitudes Toward e-Learning within a Corporate Environment Study**

Funding Source: *None.*

IRB approval #: _____

Principal investigator(s)
Mr. Steven R. Yacovelli
P.O. Box 53306
Orlando, FL 32853
(321) 217-8040

Institutional Review Board
Office of Grants and Contracts
Nova Southeastern University
(954) 262-5369

Co-investigator
Dr. Gary Anglin
University of Kentucky
137 Taylor Education Building
Lexington, KY 40506
(859) 257-5972

Description of the Study

The purpose of this study is to ask for your opinion on three different areas: (1) your attitudes toward computers; (2) your attitudes toward computer-assisted learning (sometimes called "e-learning"); and (3) your self-reported level of computer skills.

We want to know what you think regarding these three areas. Many companies are using the Internet and computers to train employees, and we want to know your opinion about this type of training delivery, what you think about computers in general, and how you would rank your own computer skills. This will help company training departments prepare classes and training that better serve you.

To find out your opinions, we will use the *Regan Computer Competence, Attitude, & Behavior Survey*. This survey asks you about the three areas. It also asks you some information about yourself and the organization where you work.

You were selected as a possible participant because you meet the two criteria of the study: (1) you are over the age of 18 years; and (2) you work within the business and/or not-for profit organization that is not an academic institution (K-12 school or college/university). This study is being conducted in partial fulfillment of the Requirements for the degree of Doctor of Education from Nova Southeastern University. We ask that you read this form and ask any questions you may have before agreeing to be in the study.

If you agree to be in this study, we would ask you following these two easy steps: (1) write in your responses to the five page *Regan Computer Competence, Attitude, & Behavior Survey*. This should take you no more than 10 to 20 minutes to complete; and you will have the chance to either fill out this survey in *paper version* or on the *computer*. The Internet address is at the end of this letter. Turn in your completed *paper survey* (if applicable) in a sealed envelop and this signed *Consent Letter* to your company's research representative.

Risks & Benefits of Being in the Study

The risk involved in this study may be minimal. The only perceived risk for this study involves the issue of confidentiality. We would make every effort to ensure that your comments are kept strictly confidential. The records of this study will be kept private. In any sort of report we might publish, we will not include any information that will make it possible to identify a participant. Research records will be stored securely and only researchers will have access to the records.

(continued)

NOVA SOUTHEASTERN UNIVERSITY
Fischler Graduate School of Education
and Human Services

While there may not be an immediate benefit to you directly, this information that you provide will help company training departments like yours prepare classes and training that better serve you.

If you have any concerns about the risks or benefits of participating in this study, you can contact Steven R. Yacovelli or Dr. Gary Anglin or the IRB Office at the numbers indicated above.

Costs & Payments to the Participant

There are no costs to you or payments made for participating in this study.

Confidentiality & Privacy

We would make every effort to ensure that your comments are kept strictly confidential. The records of this study will be kept private. In any sort of report we might publish, we will not include any information that will make it possible to identify a participant. Research records will be stored securely and only researchers will have access to the records. While you will given a "Lot Number" for tracking purposes, this number is only indicative of your organization, NOT you as an individual. All information obtained in this study is strictly confidential unless disclosure is required by law.

Use of Protected Health Information (PHI)

This study does not require the disclosure of any *Protected Health Information.*

Participant's Right to Withdraw from the Study

You have the right to withdraw at any time. If you do withdraw, it will not affect your treatment at our organization in any way. If you choose to withdraw, you may request that any data which has been collected will be destroyed unless prohibited by state or federal law.

Other Considerations

If significant new information relating to the study becomes available which may relate to your willingness to continue to participate, this information will be provided to you by the investigators.

Voluntary Consent by Participant

I have read the preceding consent form, or it has been read to me, and I fully understand the contents of this document and voluntarily consent to participate. All of my questions concerning the research have been answered. I hereby agree to participate in this research study. If I have any questions in the future about this study they will be answered Steven R. Yacovelli. A copy of this form has been given to me. This consent ends at the conclusion of this study.

Participant's Signature _____ Date _____

Authorized Representative _____ Date _____

Authority of Representative is based on: _____

Signature of Witness _____ Date _____

On-line version on the Survey is available at www.topdoglearning.biz/survey. When prompted type in LOT NUMBER _____.

1750 NE 167th Street • North Miami Beach, Florida 33162-3017 • (954) 262-8500 • 800-986-3223, ext. 8500

Appendix M

Detailed Instructions Sheet for Research Representatives

NOVA SOUTHEASTERN UNIVERSITY
Fischler Graduate School of Education
and Human Services

P.O. Box 533067
Orlando, FL 32853-3067

November 11, 2004

Hello Research Representatives:

This sheet should provide you with the details on how to distribute and collect the ***Regan Computer Competence, Attitude, and Behavior Surveys***. The process is just four simple steps:

> **STEP 1: *CONFIRM MATERIALS.*** Packet Arrives. Please send and e-mail to me (steve@topdoglearning.biz) to confirm receipt.

> **STEP 2: *DISTRIBUTION.*** Distribute <u>one</u> *Consent Form*, <u>one</u> *Paper Survey*, and <u>one</u> envelope to each volunteer.

> **STEP 3: *VOLUNTEER SELECTS MEDIA.*** At this point the volunteer reads the *Consent Form*, signs it, and decides if they want to take the *Paper Survey* or the *Online Survey* (found at **www.topdoglearning.biz/survey**). Both surveys are identical with the exception of the last question.

>> • **FYI #1:** it may take a second or two for the *Online Survey* to load, depending on your Internet connection.

>> • **FYI #2:** the *Online Survey* asks volunteers for a **LOT NUMBER** (this is printed on the bottom of their *Consent Form*). This simply allows me a way to: (1) track response rates from each organization, and (2) be able to "cut the data" by organization, if desired.

> Volunteer completes either form and submits. If they take the paper version they should placed the completed survey in the envelope and seal prior to giving back to you. Ensure that each volunteer signs the *Consent Form*!

> **STEP 4: *RETURN MATERIALS.*** Collect all *Paper Surveys* (completed or blank – I will recycle these) and signed *Consent Forms*. Be sure you signed the "witness" line of each *Consent Form*. Place these in the Pre-Paid Postage Envelope and mail to me **within two weeks of receipt**. Also please send me an e-mail to confirm that you have mailed them, so I know to look for them.

This entire process is also attached in graphic form.

If you have **ANY** questions or concerns, please feel free to call me at (321) 217-8040 at any time, or send me an e-mail at steve@topdoglearning.biz.

THANK YOU again for your help in facilitating this study, and I look forward to receiving your information within the next few weeks.

Sincerely,

Steve

PROCESS FLOW:
for distributing & collecting The Regan Computer Competence, Attitude, & Behavior Survey

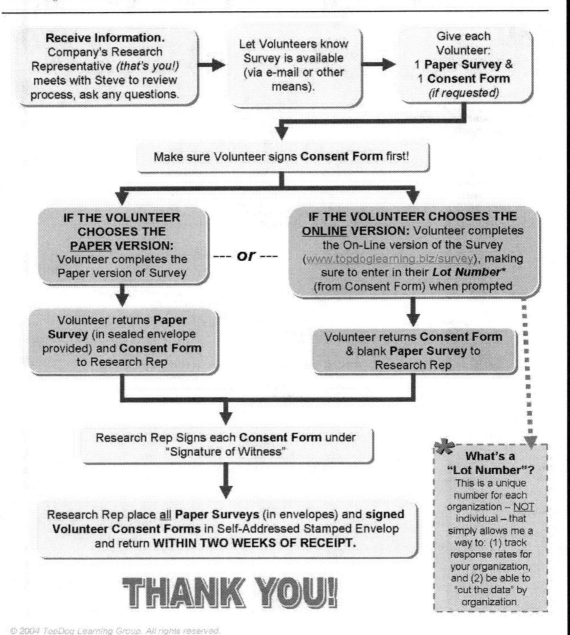

Receive Information. Company's Research Representative *(that's you!)* meets with Steve to review process, ask any questions.

Let Volunteers know Survey is available (via e-mail or other means).

Give each Volunteer: 1 **Paper Survey** & 1 **Consent Form** *(if requested)*

Make sure Volunteer signs **Consent Form** first!

IF THE VOLUNTEER CHOOSES THE <u>PAPER</u> VERSION: Volunteer completes the Paper version of Survey

--- *or* ---

IF THE VOLUNTEER CHOOSES THE <u>ONLINE</u> VERSION: Volunteer completes the On-Line version of the Survey (www.topdoglearning.biz/survey), making sure to enter in their *Lot Number** (from Consent Form) when prompted

Volunteer returns **Paper Survey** (in sealed envelope provided) and **Consent Form** to Research Rep

Volunteer returns **Consent Form** & blank **Paper Survey** to Research Rep

Research Rep Signs each **Consent Form** under "Signature of Witness"

Research Rep place <u>all</u> **Paper Surveys** (in envelopes) and **signed Volunteer Consent Forms** in Self-Addressed Stamped Envelop and return **WITHIN TWO WEEKS OF RECEIPT.**

THANK YOU!

* **What's a "Lot Number"?** This is a unique number for each organization – <u>NOT</u> individual – that simply allows me a way to: (1) track response rates for your organization, and (2) be able to "cut the data" by organization.

Appendix N

Consent Form for Representatives of the Business Organizations

NOVA SOUTHEASTERN UNIVERSITY
Fischler Graduate School of Education
and Human Services

ORGANIZATION CONSENT FORM

The Development and Use of an Instrument to Measure Adult Learner's Perceived Levels of Computer Competence, Attitudes Toward Computers, and Attitudes Toward e-Learning within a Corporate Environment

What is This Study?

You and your organization are invited participate in a research study of attitudes toward computers, computer-assisted learning, and computer skills level.

The purpose of this study is to ask members of your organization their opinions in three areas:

(1) Their attitudes toward computers;

(2) Their attitudes toward computer-assisted learning (sometimes called "e-learning"); and

(3) Their self-reported level of computer skills.

We want to know what your employees think regarding these three areas. Many companies are using the Internet and computers to train employees, and we want to know your employees' opinion about this type of training delivery, what they think about computers in general, and how they rank their own computer skills. This will help company training departments prepare classes and training that better serve its employees.

To find out their opinions, we will use the **Regan Computer Competence, Attitude, & Behavior Survey**, a 5-page survey developed by Steven Yacovelli. Completion of the survey should only take approximately 10-20 minutes. This survey asks about the three areas listed above, and some basic demographic information about the employees and their respective work organization.

(Please complete the following section as well, which will be sent as part of the degree requirements of Nova Southeastern University).

Applied Research Office
Nova Southeastern University
1750 NE 167th Street
North Miami Beach, FL 33162

To: University IRB Office:

As an authorized representative of _____ *(your organization)*, I have given Mr. Steven R. Yacovelli permission to conduct his research in our organization. I understand the scope of his research and how he will collect and present the data gathered. All information to be gathered will be done in a confidential and appropriate manner. I further understand that Mr. Yacovelli's study is expected to run from November 2004 and January 2005.

At no time will Mr. Yacovelli's research be used in a way that would have potential risk to subjects or participants from my organization.

Should you have any questions, please feel free to contact me.

Sincerely,

_____   _____
Signature   Date

_____
Printed Name

_____   _____
Title   Daytime Phone

1750 NE 167th Street • North Miami Beach, Florida 33162-3017 • (954) 262-8500 • 800-986-3223, ext. 8500

Appendix O

Item-to-Subtotal Correlations Construct Validity for the Regan CCABS for

Section 3: Self-Reported Computer Competence

Item-to-Subtotal Correlations Construct Validity for the Regan CCABS for Section 3: Self-Reported Computer Competence

		Section 3: Self-Reported Computer Competence Subtotal
Section 3: Self-Reported Computer Competence Subtotal	Pearson Correlation	1
	Sig. (2-tailed)	.
	N	144
Q11 - I own a computer	Pearson Correlation	.50 (**)
	Sig. (2-tailed)	0
Q12 - I am good at using computers	Pearson Correlation	.75 (**)
	Sig. (2-tailed)	0
Q13 - I know what an operating system is	Pearson Correlation	.69 (**)
	Sig. (2-tailed)	0
Q14 - I know what a database is	Pearson Correlation	.68 (**)
	Sig. (2-tailed)	0
Q15 - I know how to install software on a personal computer	Pearson Correlation	.76 (**)
	Sig. (2-tailed)	0
Q16 - I know how to write computer programs	Pearson Correlation	.36 (**)
	Sig. (2-tailed)	0
Q17 - I know what a LAN is	Pearson Correlation	.64 (**)
	Sig. (2-tailed)	0
Q18 - I often use a mainframe computer system	Pearson Correlation	.24 (**)
	Sig. (2-tailed)	0.004
Q19 - I know how to recover deleted or "lost data" on a PC or computer	Pearson Correlation	.50 (**)
	Sig. (2-tailed)	0
Q20 - I have Internet access at home	Pearson Correlation	.51 (**)

	Sig. (2-tailed)	0
Q21 - When I come across a topic I do not know or understand, I first consult the Internet for information	Pearson Correlation	.55 (**)
	Sig. (2-tailed)	0
Q22 - I am comfortable with on-line business transactions (like checking my bank statements or paying my credit card bills on-	Pearson Correlation	.55 (**)
	Sig. (2-tailed)	0
Q23 - I have purchased something through the Internet (like airline tickets, movie tickets, items bought through eBay®)	Pearson Correlation	.55 (**)
	Sig. (2-tailed)	0
Q24 - I have used a computer for learning something new (like finding a new recipe or how to fix a broken VCR)	Pearson Correlation	.66 (**)
	Sig. (2-tailed)	0
Q25 - I know what e-mail is	Pearson Correlation	.61 (**)
	Sig. (2-tailed)	0
Q26 - I have a personal e-mail account	Pearson Correlation	.56 (**)
	Sig. (2-tailed)	0
Q27 - I use e-mail more often to communicate with family and friends than I do through standard letters	Pearson Correlation	.60 (**)
	Sig. (2-tailed)	0
Q28 - I have participated in a "chat room"	Pearson Correlation	.52 (**)
	Sig. (2-tailed)	0
Q29 - I regularly use a PC or computer for word processing	Pearson Correlation	.58 (**)
	Sig. (2-tailed)	0
Q30 - I have used an Automated Teller Machine (ATM)	Pearson Correlation	.38 (**)
	Sig. (2-tailed)	0
Q31 - I know how to save and print pictures from a digital camera	Pearson Correlation	.68 (**)
	Sig. (2-tailed)	0

Q32 - I use a Palm Pilot® or other type of Personal Digital Assistant (PDA) frequently	Pearson Correlation	.30 (**)
	Sig. (2-tailed)	0
Q33 - I frequently read computer magazines or other sources of information that describe new computer technology	Pearson Correlation	.49 (**)
	Sig. (2-tailed)	0
Q34 - I consider myself to be computer literate	Pearson Correlation	.76 (**)
	Sig. (2-tailed)	0
Q35 - I am comfortable … reading, sending and deleting e-mail messages	Pearson Correlation	.64 (**)
	Sig. (2-tailed)	0
Q36 - I am comfortable … sending and reading e-mail attachments	Pearson Correlation	.60 (**)
	Sig. (2-tailed)	0
Q37 - I feel comfortable … following threaded discussions and posting messages on bulletin boards on the computer	Pearson Correlation	.75 (**)
	Sig. (2-tailed)	0
Q38 - I feel comfortable … participating in chat sessions	Pearson Correlation	.60 (**)
	Sig. (2-tailed)	0
Q39 - I feel comfortable … installing the latest version of a browser such as Internet Explorer® or Netscape®	Pearson Correlation	.74 (**)
	Sig. (2-tailed)	0
Q40 - I feel comfortable … locating and installing plugins such as Shockwave®, Quicktime®, or VRML	Pearson Correlation	.72 (**)
	Sig. (2-tailed)	0
Q41 - I feel comfortable … creating Web pages with images, links, and text	Pearson Correlation	.55 (**)
	Sig. (2-tailed)	0
Q42 - I feel comfortable … following links on Web pages and returning to the starting point	Pearson Correlation	.67 (**)
	Sig. (2-tailed)	0

Q43 - I feel comfortable ... recognizing clickable objects on Web pages	Pearson Correlation	.71 (**)
	Sig. (2-tailed)	0
Q44 - I feel comfortable ... downloading files embedded on Web pages	Pearson Correlation	.78 (**)
	Sig. (2-tailed)	0
Q45 - I feel comfortable ... knowing what a PDF file is	Pearson Correlation	.70 (**)
	Sig. (2-tailed)	0
Q46 - I am comfortable ... opening files with Adobe Acrobat®	Pearson Correlation	.65 (**)
	Sig. (2-tailed)	0
Q47 - I am comfortable ... printing one or more pages from Adobe Acrobat®	Pearson Correlation	.67 (**)
	Sig. (2-tailed)	0
Q48 - I am comfortable ... opening a compressed file (sometimes called a ZIP file)	Pearson Correlation	.74 (**)
	Sig. (2-tailed)	0
Q49 - I am comfortable ... moving files to different drives within my computer	Pearson Correlation	.74 (**)
	Sig. (2-tailed)	0
Q50 - Overall, I would consider myself to be competent with computers	Pearson Correlation	.81 (**)
	Sig. (2-tailed)	0

Note. CCABS = Regan Computer Competence, Attitude, and Behavior Survey. *Correlation is significant at the 0.05 level (2-tailed). **Correlation is significant at the 0.01 level (2-tailed).

Appendix P

Item-to-Subtotal Correlations Construct Validity for the Regan CCABS for

Section 4: Attitudes Toward Computers

Item-to-Subtotal Correlations Construct Validity for the Regan CCABS for Section 4: Attitudes Toward Computers

		Section 4: Attitudes toward Computers Subtotal
Section 4: Attitudes toward Computers Subtotal	Pearson Correlation	1
	Sig. (2-tailed)	.
	N	144
Q51 - Computers do not scare me at all	Pearson Correlation	.79 (**)
	Sig. (2-tailed)	0
Q52 - I get anxious when I think of trying to use a computer	Pearson Correlation	.46 (**)
	Sig. (2-tailed)	0
Q53 - I'm no good with computers	Pearson Correlation	.49 (**)
	Sig. (2-tailed)	0
Q54 - I am sure I could learn a computer language	Pearson Correlation	.48 (**)
	Sig. (2-tailed)	0
Q55 - It wouldn't bother me at all to take computer courses	Pearson Correlation	.73 (**)
	Sig. (2-tailed)	0
Q56 - Computers make me feel uncomfortable	Pearson Correlation	.63 (**)
	Sig. (2-tailed)	0
Q57 - Working with a computer would make me very nervous	Pearson Correlation	.60 (**)
	Sig. (2-tailed)	0
Q58 - I would feel at ease in a computer class	Pearson Correlation	.66 (**)
	Sig. (2-tailed)	0
Q59 - I would feel comfortable working with a computer	Pearson Correlation	.72 (**)
	Sig. (2-tailed)	0
Q60 - I'm not the type to do well with computers	Pearson Correlation	.73 (**)
	Sig. (2-tailed)	0

Q61 - I do not feel threatened when others talk about computers	Pearson Correlation	.47 (**)
	Sig. (2-tailed)	0
Q62 - Generally, I would feel OK about trying a new problem on the computer	Pearson Correlation	.76 (**)
	Sig. (2-tailed)	0
Q63 - I don't think I would do advanced computer work	Pearson Correlation	.52 (**)
	Sig. (2-tailed)	0
Q64 - Computers make me feel uneasy and confused	Pearson Correlation	.71 (**)
	Sig. (2-tailed)	0
Q65 - I am sure I could do work with computers	Pearson Correlation	.56 (**)
	Sig. (2-tailed)	0
Q66 - I feel aggressive and hostile toward computers	Pearson Correlation	.65 (**)
	Sig. (2-tailed)	0
Q67 - I think using a computer would be very hard for me	Pearson Correlation	.54 (**)
	Sig. (2-tailed)	0
Q68 - I would be successful in computer training courses	Pearson Correlation	.75 (**)
	Sig. (2-tailed)	0
Q69 - I do not think I could handle a computer course	Pearson Correlation	.59 (**)
	Sig. (2-tailed)	0
Q70 - I have a lot of self-confidence when it comes to working with computers	Pearson Correlation	.84 (**)
	Sig. (2-tailed)	0
Q71 - I would like working with computers	Pearson Correlation	.79 (**)
	Sig. (2-tailed)	0
Q72 - The challenge of solving problems with computers does not appeal to me	Pearson Correlation	.69 (**)
	Sig. (2-tailed)	0
Q73 - I think working with computers would be enjoyable and stimulating	Pearson Correlation	.76 (**)
	Sig. (2-tailed)	0

Q74 - Figuring out computer problems does not appeal to me	Pearson Correlation	.70 (**)
	Sig. (2-tailed)	0
Q75 - When there is a problem with a computer run that I can't immediately solve, I would stick with it until I have the answer	Pearson Correlation	.69 (**)
	Sig. (2-tailed)	0
Q76 - I don't understand how some people can spend so much time working with computers and seem to enjoy it.	Pearson Correlation	.68 (**)
	Sig. (2-tailed)	0
Q77 - Once I start to work with the computer, I would find it hard to stop	Pearson Correlation	.61 (**)
	Sig. (2-tailed)	0
Q78 - I will do as little work with computers as possible	Pearson Correlation	.66 (**)
	Sig. (2-tailed)	0
Q79 - If a problem is left unsolved in a computer training class, I would continue to think about it afterward	Pearson Correlation	.65 (**)
	Sig. (2-tailed)	0
Q80 - I do not enjoy talking with others about computers	Pearson Correlation	.66 (**)
	Sig. (2-tailed)	0
Q81 - I use computers many ways in my life	Pearson Correlation	.71 (**)
	Sig. (2-tailed)	0
Q82 - Learning about computers is a waste of time	Pearson Correlation	.68 (**)
	Sig. (2-tailed)	0
Q83 - Learning about computers is worthwhile	Pearson Correlation	.59 (**)
	Sig. (2-tailed)	0
Q84 - I need a firm mastery of computers for my work	Pearson Correlation	.48 (**)
	Sig. (2-tailed)	0
Q85 - I have little use for computers in my daily life	Pearson Correlation	.51 (**)
	Sig. (2-tailed)	0
Q86 - I can't think of any way that I use computers in my career	Pearson Correlation	.56 (**)

	Sig. (2-tailed)	0
Q87 - Knowing how to work with computers will increase my job possibilities	Pearson Correlation	.55 (**)
	Sig. (2-tailed)	0
Q88 - Anything that a computer can be used for, I can do just as well some other way	Pearson Correlation	.31 (**)
	Sig. (2-tailed)	0
Q89 - It is important to me to do well in computer training courses	Pearson Correlation	.57 (**)
	Sig. (2-tailed)	0
Q90 - Working with computers is not important to me in my life's work	Pearson Correlation	.59 (**)
	Sig. (2-tailed)	0
Q91 - Computers cause more trouble than they are worth	Pearson Correlation	.69 (**)
	Sig. (2-tailed)	0
Q92 - People who don't know how to use a computer cannot function in modern society	Pearson Correlation	.26 (**)
	Sig. (2-tailed)	0.002
Q93 - I find computers to be vital to my everyday life	Pearson Correlation	.62 (**)
	Sig. (2-tailed)	0
Q94 - I enjoy working on a computer	Pearson Correlation	.79 (**)
	Sig. (2-tailed)	0
Q95 - Computers are too difficult to use	Pearson Correlation	.69 (**)
	Sig. (2-tailed)	0
Q96 - I usually get frustrated using a computer	Pearson Correlation	.69 (**)
	Sig. (2-tailed)	0
Q97 - I can use a computer to accomplish what I want	Pearson Correlation	.70 (**)
	Sig. (2-tailed)	0
Q98 - I feel computers are valuable tools in people's personal and professional lives	Pearson Correlation	.60 (**)
	Sig. (2-tailed)	0

Q99 - Computers serve little use in my life	Pearson Correlation	.49 (**)
	Sig. (2-tailed)	0
Q100 - I think computers are better left used by office workers and "younger" people	Pearson Correlation	.60 (**)
	Sig. (2-tailed)	0

Note. CCABS = Regan Computer Competence, Attitude, and Behavior Survey. *Correlation is significant at the 0.05 level (2-tailed). **Correlation is significant at the 0.01 level (2-tailed).

Appendix Q

Item-to-Subtotal Correlations Construct Validity for the Regan CCABS for

Section 5: Attitudes Toward e-Learning

Item-to-Subtotal Correlations Construct Validity for the Regan CCABS for Section 5: Attitudes Toward e-Learning

		Section 5: Attitudes toward e-Learning Subtotal
Section 5: Attitudes toward e-Learning Subtotal	Pearson Correlation	1
	Sig. (2-tailed)	.
	N	144
Q101 - I am sure I could do well in an Internet-delivered course	Pearson Correlation	.58 (**)
	Sig. (2-tailed)	0
Q102 - I am not the type to do well with computers	Pearson Correlation	.62 (**)
	Sig. (2-tailed)	0
Q103 - Taking an Internet-delivered training class would be one way to stay current with new technology	Pearson Correlation	.63 (**)
	Sig. (2-tailed)	0
Q104 - Internet-delivered training classes provide an efficient way for me to utilize my time	Pearson Correlation	.69 (**)
	Sig. (2-tailed)	0
Q105 - I would be upset if a required training class were only offered over the Internet	Pearson Correlation	.73 (**)
	Sig. (2-tailed)	0
Q106 - I feel at ease using the Internet (or "Web")	Pearson Correlation	.36 (**)
	Sig. (2-tailed)	0
Q107 - I feel that technology gets in the way of learning content	Pearson Correlation	.54 (**)
	Sig. (2-tailed)	0
Q108 - If I had a choice between taking an Internet training class or a "traditional" face to face section of the same class I	Pearson Correlation	.72 (**)
	Sig. (2-tailed)	0
Q109 - If I took a training class delivered over the Internet, I would feel isolated	Pearson Correlation	.76 (**)
	Sig. (2-tailed)	0
Q110 - I feel that Internet-delivered training classes provide a greater opportunity for interactivity between students, and be	Pearson Correlation	.61 (**)

	Sig. (2-tailed)	0
Q111 - I would be anxious about taking an Internet-delivered training class	Pearson Correlation	.52 (**)
	Sig. (2-tailed)	0
Q112 - I would be excited to take a training class delivered over the Internet	Pearson Correlation	.84 (**)
	Sig. (2-tailed)	0
Q113 - If I took a training class delivered via the Internet, it would be a chance to learn about the Internet	Pearson Correlation	.60 (**)
	Sig. (2-tailed)	0
Q114 - I feel that Internet-delivered training classes are impersonal	Pearson Correlation	.65 (**)
	Sig. (2-tailed)	0
Q115 - Access would be a problem if I took an Internet-delivered training class	Pearson Correlation	.51 (**)
	Sig. (2-tailed)	0
Q116 - Taking an Internet-delivered training class would be a good way to learn	Pearson Correlation	.80 (**)
	Sig. (2-tailed)	0
Q117 - It would be convenient for me to take an Internet-delivered training class	Pearson Correlation	.69 (**)
	Sig. (2-tailed)	0
Q118 - I think using a computer for a training class would be very hard for me	Pearson Correlation	.62 (**)
	Sig. (2-tailed)	0
Q119 - I would find it hard to motivate myself if I were to take a training class using the Internet	Pearson Correlation	.72 (**)
	Sig. (2-tailed)	0
Q120 - Internet-delivered training classes are an efficient way to deliver training	Pearson Correlation	.72 (**)
	Sig. (2-tailed)	0
Q121 - It's better to attend a training class with an instructor than gain the same information from a computer	Pearson Correlation	.68 (**)
	Sig. (2-tailed)	0
Q122 - I could learn just as well from an Internet-delivered course as I could from a "traditional" training class	Pearson Correlation	.76 (**)
	Sig. (2-tailed)	0
Q123 - I would like the flexibility of attending an Internet-delivered training class	Pearson Correlation	.78 (**)
	Sig. (2-tailed)	0

Q124 - Communicating online with classmates in Internet-delivered courses would be an enhancement to learning	Pearson Correlation	.67 (**)
	Sig. (2-tailed)	0
Q125 - I would feel uneasy if I had to take an Internet-delivered training class	Pearson Correlation	.73 (**)
	Sig. (2-tailed)	0
Q126 - Training delivered over the Internet is too impersonal	Pearson Correlation	.73 (**)
	Sig. (2-tailed)	0
Q127 - I feel an Internet-delivered training course would allow more interaction between students, and between the students and	Pearson Correlation	.67 (**)
	Sig. (2-tailed)	0
Q128 - The use of technology can enhance the learning in a training course	Pearson Correlation	.63 (**)
	Sig. (2-tailed)	0
Q129 - I would be eager to take a training class delivered over the Internet	Pearson Correlation	.80 (**)
	Sig. (2-tailed)	0
Q130 - If I were to take a training class delivered over the Internet, I would find it hard to complete the class	Pearson Correlation	.57 (**)
	Sig. (2-tailed)	0

Note. CCABS = Regan Computer Competence, Attitude, and Behavior Survey. *Correlation is significant at the 0.05 level (2-tailed). **Correlation is significant at the 0.01 level (2-tailed).

www.ingramcontent.com/pod-product-compliance
Lightning Source LLC
Chambersburg PA
CBHW060555060326
40690CB00017B/3716